MEHDI

MY RESCUE STORY

MEDHI JOUMAZADEH

AFGHAN REFUGEE
SCAPE TO FREEDOM

DEDICATE THIS BOOK TO

To my wonderful and faith-filled wife Jeyran

i know if it wasnot because of my wife i wouldnot be here today standing and writing this book, this is happening just because of her encoragment and love that she expressed to me, i am going to dedicate tis book to my lovely wife jeyran my kids gabe and radmila and my mom and my sisters sharifeh golestani, mahnaz and mahboubeh joumazadeh, all my friends, around the world that helped me to be who i am now,i came here into united state with hope that i can find peacfull life and without my wife and each of my friends none of them were possible, i wanna thanks especially to neal and tisha headway , aron& megan keyes, amir & bahar shahabi ,sam and ezer, vahid noruzi, pastor mark and cherry, pastor vinny & ariel, fred and deena osborn, bob & marry mulloy, david & kristen okada, danniel & sky whang, sister marta masrori, maryam ranjbar, fred milani, has-

san and nahid ebrahimi, mrs dawn fondy, steve, betsy&
britt, jeff and karlla reinhart, tod and kim golden, elliza-
beth & jason, michaela and her family, serah & david,
justin & kristin moor, tony & kim Mcwhorter, bart &
collen galsgow, chris & grace vollo, kai & mchelle omar,
kyl & amy johnson,josh & rebekah smith, mark & sandy,
sandy & david, my afghan faitfull brother and sisters,
latif & samira, banfshe, atefeh, somaye, enayat&arzo
mahdavi, ali and aghele, soghra and hamid, annam and
marria, brother hossein and shahnaz ebrahimi, kambiz &
asrin, fatemeh & mohammad gholami, mohmmad &
soozan ghambin, milad and yoonia, hosseyn &
symin,shahrzad & aref,

i know this list need to be longer and just i wanna say
thankyou so much to every one isnot in this list, and if i
missed your name forgive me but just i want you let you
know you always be in our heart and my god bless you
for being good friend and support my wife and kids when
i wsnot here in usa and after that, we love you and al-
ways

mehdi & jeyarn

FORWARDED BY NEAL HADAWAY

An Anything Good Come from Nazareth?

This was the question that Nathanael asked when Philip told him, "We have found the one Moses wrote about in the Law, and about whom the prophets also wrote—Jesus of Nazareth, the son of Joseph" (John 1:45). Philip wanted his friend to meet Jesus, so his answer was simple: "Come and see" (v.46), and they went together to see Jesus.

Have you ever been so sure of one opinion that you almost missed seeing the truth or missed receiving a blessing? Do our pre-conceived ideas or our pre-judgments (prejudices) prevent us from seeing others as God sees them? We live in an exciting time when globalization is growing rapidly & it seems the world is shrinking. People & nations are now connected and inter-connected worldwide more than ever before, and it increases daily, but many times our relationships seem less personal. There is more 'connectedness' through internet & social media now than ever before, but we're also more isolated & self-absorbed.

Maybe part of our problem is that we have difficulty understanding the difference between Spiritual and Physical.

It seems that Jesus spent much of His time with His disciples helping them to discern the importance of spiritual realities and not to let the physical (and therefore temporary) distract them from the eternal. They had to learn many difficult lessons that we, if we are wise, will seek to learn from the Master also.

How do you feel about the current worldwide refugee situation? Do we see it as a problem or as an opportunity? What are the issues surrounding/ involved with refugees here in our own country? What exactly is a refugee? And why are they here? What is my responsibility? What do they need and how can we help? What would God have me to do?

Can't I just ignore the problems & hope that everything will turn out right? How can I pray effectively for the needs of refugees & be a part of God's solutions? How can I partner w/ organizations or programs in a meaningful way?

There are more Muslims coming to Christ now than ever before. The world is coming to us, and we're called to reach them with the Good News of Jesus. I've known Mehdi ever since he arrived in the USA four years ago. His story is unique, but it's also very similar to many other refugees worldwide who flee from violence, war & persecution to seek safety in 'safer' countries. And as they find safety & freedom for their families in welcoming countries, they are also able to hear & respond to the true message of Jesus the Messiah:

- He is the Messiah the Old Testament prophets pointed toward

- He was the perfect, sinless sacrifice for the sins of the world

- He died a criminal's death, but was raised to new & eternal life on the 3rd day

- This Messiah is the perfect Prophet, Priest & King who brings peace into the hearts & lives of all who will receive him

- And just as Jesus the Messiah is our Living Sacrifice, he calls each of us who follow him to live our lives as His living sacrifices.

You might ask: Can anything good come from Afghanistan? Or from Syria? Or Iran or Iraq? Come and see. Listen to the stories of refugees who flee destruction, looking for a new life in a blessed land. Come and see what God is doing in the hearts & lives of the down-trodden and how He is fulfilling his promise to Abraham that through him, 'all peoples on earth will be blessed' (Genesis 12:3). *"The King will reply, 'Truly I tell you, whatever you did for one of the least of these brothers & sisters of mine, you did for Me.'"* (Matthew 25:40)

CONTENTS

1. Realizing Who i am? 1

2. Planing my future. 7

3. journey of life and death 24

4. Endless Rout. 36

5. Become a Human Smuggler 47

6. Taste of Money 57

7. Seeking Freedom 68

8. See My Mother Again 82

9. Back to Work 92

10. An Unexpected Guest in the Church 102

11. Freedom Ticket 119

12. Real Face of Europ 128

13. God Changed My Plans 144

14. Running For My Life 158

15. Become a Official Refugee 174

16. Finding My Life Partner 190

17. Hardest Desicion in My Life 207

18. Become a Father 220

19. Seeing My Doughter First Time 239

20. Become Citizens of Heaven 258

Editor's Note 266

CHAPTER ONE

REALIZING WHO I AM?

I come from a very poor Afghan family. As a small child my shoes were always torn, and we had no money to replace them. My father had undergone back surgery that made it too painful for him to work at any job that required heavy manual labor. My mom had a weak heart and needed heart surgery, but we could not afford it. Poverty was our identity. We lived in a single room at the end of the big yard of a rich man's house. My mom took care of the household chores, while my dad was tending the garden at his house. The owner was a rich, but he was stingy old man; he even kept a count of the figs on the trees to make sure no one except him ate them.

1

I remember one beautiful March morning I was walking with my dad. I was six years old and my dad took my picture to remember that day because it was my first day at school. I was all excited and impatient to see my first class. It was a different school from the rest in our neighborhood. It was only for international students – not for the local Iranians.

It was only my first day at school, and already I started fighting with one of my classmates. I was jealous of him because was one of the coolest and handsomest kids in my class. He was tall with blonde hair and blue eyes. After few minutes, the principal arrived, stopped the fight, and took us both to his office. He asked us to shake hands and be friends. I asked my classmate's name, and he said "Give." I've never known such a name before. However, after that day we became friends and sat next to each other in the back bench.

One day his mom came to pick him up from school and she offered me a ride which I gladly accepted. I had never been in a personal car before. So, it was the first time I got to ride in an automobile other than public bus or school bus. It was not a fancy car; it was an old, surplus Jeep Wrangler left-over from America's Vietnam war era. It was a beat up car with no roof and doors, but I liked it. I thoroughly enjoyed the ride. His mom was talking to me in her accent, but I wasn't paying attention as I was overwhelmed with the joy of sitting in a car. The breeze was blowing my hair and getting into my ears. As the car pickup speed, I opened my mouth to get as much fresh air as I could (who knew if I could ever get this chance again). As they dropped me off at my house, Give's mom started talking to my mom with an expectation to make friends with us. But my mom was not interested as she considered Give's mom an American infidel.

But, Give and I became real good friends and were together in everything including going to and from school. He was living just two streets away from my home and so, I used to go to their big house every day. I was excited to go to their house every single day because their refrigerator was always full of food. You could eat as much fruit as you wanted, and nobody would count them. In the big house you could run everywhere, yet nobody said anything. But those happy days of my life did not last long. Our landlord passed away and his son wanted to sell the house. So, we had no choice but, to leave. We had to move to another city far from that place. My dad got a new job in a big garden; his job was to take care of the trees, open and close the gate and guard the property to make sure nobody stole the fruits.

We had to live in a broken down RV for almost a year. My mom had to cook outside because there was no kitchen, and there was no bathroom too. I did not know why we were stuck there. Our last home was much better. At least we had a bathroom and my mom could cook inside the house; there was no dust and no rust. I noticed that my mother's hands were getting older all the time, and I could see her skin starting to wrinkle and scale. I asked myself why Give's mom could drive her own car, had big expensive house and everything that we did not have, but my mom had to live in this situation: with no money, and living with so much suffering.

I found another way to go visit Give's house. I had to ride four different buses, and it took me five hours to get there, but I was okay with that. Every Thursday morning, I would get ready to leave for Give's and Friday night I would come back home. When I was going, I was so excited, but on the way back home I was not happy at all. I did not like to say goodbye and walk away from what had become my dream home – the place where I could play and enjoy life without seeing my family suffer. Sometimes I only had a couple hours to play with him, but I felt it was worth the five hours to get there and the same amount of time to return home.

One time, I was invited to stay at their house for three days and four nights. Talking with Give during that visit, I explained to him everything my family was going through and asked him why we are like this, but his family was different. "When I'm with you, I realize we are poor." I asked, "is this our fault or because of something else?" He did not have an answer, but told me, "If you want to come to visit old church in tehran with us." I accepted, and we went together to church. When I stepped inside the church, I felt that place was so different from our place where we were going to pray. Everybody was quiet and nobody was hitting themselves. As I looked around, I saw candles burning everywhere. It was a completely different atmosphere from our place of worship.

When I came back home from that visit, I started to explain everything we did with my mom, but she immediately freaked out and told me I must not go their house again. But I would deceive my mother and go there sometimes to visit with him. But these happy times would come to an end soon. Although I was willing to sacrifice my time and energy to ride the bus and visit my friend every day, that sacrifice was not enough. My friend had reached military age, but he did not want to become a soldier in the Iranian army. And the only way he could avoid being pressed into military service was to leave the country.

When the day finally came for Give and his family to depart, I went to the airport to say goodbye to my friend once again. But this time I knew there was no bus I could ride on to follow where my friend was going. i wishe it was.

As my friend turned and waved goodbye to me, I did not know when or where we would ever see each other again. I was trying to remember every second I spent with Give, and it was at that moment that all my dreams fell apart.

CHAPTER TWO

PLANING MY FUTURE.

After Give and his family left, I was heart-sick for almost a month. I could not eat and play or communicate with anybody. But I realized I had to move on and start my own life without my best friend. I started working in a cloth fabrication plant. I learned that job very fast. It was not because I was talented or just because we needed money to survive, but every time I looked at my mother's hands I was motivated to work harder and learn faster.

At that time all my young friends and family wanted to go Europe or Australia, if possible. I felt that Europe or England would be a good option for me maybe i can see give again, because my uncle was there. Although reaching England would be a hard and dangerous journey, it would be worth it to go instead of staying in Iran and suffering without any hope for a better future. All the stories friends and family were telling me were convincing me and tempting me to go, but my big challenge was how could I tell my family I was going, especially my mom. I knew she would not like me going; I was the only hope she had.

It was known that the route from Iran to Europe is extremely dangerous for poor refugees to follow. Everyone who considered this route knew that some families had lost their children on this journey and some disappeared, never to be found again. Many others who tried to make this journey were captured or killed by terrorists or even iranian border plice shot them to death, Some people were lost at sea and drowned in the ocean when they attempted to cross over water into Europe. Still, my mind was made up to go and I started counting down every second until I would leave Iran to find my future in a faraway country and see my friend again.

I had a friend who was preparing to go, and we were planning to leave together, but I had to wait to convince my family to let me go. So, when his turn came, he had to leave without me. But I was in contact with the same smuggler who took him to Turkey and arranged to have him send me on the same route my friend had taken. For $1,000 dollars, he would arrange a passport and transportation all the way to Istanbul. However, we did not have that kind of money, so we had to travel the hard way on foot over the mountains and sneak through the border. We agreed to the price of $200, which would be paid by my father to the smuggler once I safely arrived at my destination.

He explained everything that I would need to know about the way we were going. He told me we needed to walk almost five days and six nights and to be prepared for the extremely cold weather. We would be led by local guides that were part of his network of smugglers. I would have to carry enough food for almost a week. All was the same as my friend had told me. I followed all the smuggler's instructions and prepared everything I would need for the long trek out of Iran. I took with me what little money I had managed to save from working at the textile factory. At last, the day came for me to leave my family behind and depart for an unknown destination.

I knew my mom had a tender heart. She was very sad and started crying from the day I told her I wanted to go. The moment the car came to pick me up, she looked into my eyes; her hands were shaking, and her chin started to quiver. I knew what she is feeling. She had a very hard life, raising kids with no money and had to work with my dad every step of the way. She was a strong woman, but this was the life of a afghan refugee and she was committed to live like this without complaint.

My foreign nationality caused me to be insulted and discriminated against in iran. Because I was the child of refugees from Afghanistan, I was prohibited from attending school in Iran. My foreign tongue and the shape of my eyes immediately set me apart as not belonging to that place. But I felt that because I was an immigrant, I could be wherever I wanted to be and maybe that is the good part of being an immigrant. It gave me the courage to leave Iran and seek a better life somewhere else. My heart was breaking that day, but I finally said good-bye to my family. We left each other's company with tears in our eyes, but I promised my parents that someday and one day I would come back and we would all see each other again.

When I arrived at the smuggler's house, he opened the door and greeted us. I came inside the yard and all around me I saw backpacks. I quickly realized that almost 70 Afghans were there. They were all ready to go and for the same reasons, but with different destinations. Once I sat down, they started talking with me, sharing their own experiences and stories, and giving me advice. The man in charge of the smuggling operation approached me and introduced me to a group of twelve people that would need to leave together. Two cars came to the front door and they called us to get into them. I liked the way they were doing things. It was really organized and managed well. All was on a good schedule and was done systematically.

Before we left the big house, they brought out a big sheep and sacrificed it for our protection and put some of the sheep's blood on our back packs. I thought it was very strange to sacrifice a sheep to god to protect us when we were trying to do something illegal by entering another country without permission. I did not understand the concept, but everybody else liked it. At last, the time came for us to get into a big bus and start our journey out of Iran. As soon as I sat down, the other Afghans on the bus started fighting in the middle of the bus. I was not surprised because this is the Afghan style of traveling. It seems that Afghans cannot travel without fighting; it is a kind of medicine we need to take to relieve the stress.

The guy beside me who started all the arguing and fighting introduced himself. His name was ahmad. He spoke with a strange accent, as he told me that he was trying to teach the young guys how to behave and listen to him. I asked him who he was and why they needed to listen to him. He told me he was in this business and this was the sixth time he was going this way. "I know a lot," he boasted, "and I have a lot of experience. You should listen to me." I thought he seemed too boastful and I didn't think he was right about what he was saying.

I could not sleep much that night on the bus. Once, I fell into a deep sleep, but after a couple of hours the bus driver's helper shook me and woke me up. He told me we needed to get out of the bus and change into a car. I saw a couple of hired cars waiting for us. I got into one of the cars and we traveled for about three hours before we came near the first police station on the way to the border. At first, we were very scared, but the taxi driver asked us to try sleeping, or at least to fake sleep. We did, and police did not pay any attention to us as we passed by their station. It was dark, when we arrived at the desert area near the border. They moved us from the cars into a house. As soon as I opened the door, the strong smell from within bothered my nose. There was a strong stench of human sweat inside, but I was used to it because every place I had worked, men would sit together and labor in close quarters.

ahmad told me that all the men sleeping in this house were refugees and we were all doing the same thing. As we entered the room, he kicked their asses and told them to wake up and stand up. I was surprised to see them all get up and move without any complaint. I could see the fear in their eyes and felt bad for them. I wondered how long this fear had been in their eyes,i see this fear in my self to,living in this country make me feel unworthy, why it needed to be there, and if it needed to be in my eyes too. I wondered why we needed to fear these people. ahmad asked them to give us blankets and space so we can sleep, and they did so without any resistance. I soon learned that ahmad knew what he is doing. He was different from the other guys; I could see in his eyes that he was truly confident and brave. They all fell back asleep, but I was too restless to allow sleep to envelop my mind. I was thinking all night about my future and about my family. When would I come back and see my family again? Can I bring happiness and comfort into their lives? Was I their only hope for a better future?

It was still the middle of the night when I heard footsteps outside. They were talking in Kurdish, but I could understand that something was wrong. The homeowner came inside and called us, "Wake up! Wake up! Police are coming." We had to move fast and leave the house before they arrived. We jumped into a truck and the driver started going very fast. There was no asphalt road beneath us. We were on an old, rough, dusty road and at every turn or bump we were hitting against the metal walls of the truck. It was a very hard night for all of us. We had to focus on the dark road ahead and just pray the driver did not make any mistakes that would cost us our lives.

Finally, we reached the point where we could stop and get out of the truck. As soon as we stepped out of the truck another incident happened that reminded us of the dangerous journey we were on. Once we were all out of the truck, we heard a shot ring out. Someone nearby was shooting bullets at us. The driver did not hesitate a moment, pressed on the gas pedal and disappeared in a cloud of dust. I was very scared. And even though ahmad had been on this route before, he too was confused and frightened by the gunfire. I asked him what we should do, but he could not answer. Just then I heard a voice calling our names and realized he was the smuggler we should be following. After a couple of minutes, the shooting was over, and it was safe for us to come out of hiding and gather around this smuggler who led us onward.

We walked until sunup. The smuggler told us to wait in the narrow valley we were in until that night. They promised to return to pick us up and lead us to the next stop on our trek to the border.

While we waited for night to come again, the sun was bearing down on us. There was no shade for us to take refuge and the temperatures were getting hotter and hotter as the day wore on. It became clear to me that we did not bring enough water with us and we would be in trouble soon. It was still the first day and we had five more days of walking ahead of us. I was starting to worry about what would happen to us and how we could survive if we stayed hot and thirsty like this the entire way.

After a few hours of waiting, two men came and approached us. They demanded more money from us, or they would not take us any farther from where we were. Before I started on this journey, I spoke with the smuggler who arranged this trip and told him I would not pay any more money to anyone until I arrived in Istanbul. He gave me his 100% guarantee that no more money would be paid to anyone along the way. I did not know who these men were, and they knew nothing of any guarantees given to me or anyone else. So, when they started threatening our group to force us to pay them money, I boldly told them I would not pay them any money. When I told them that I didn't have money to pay them, one of the men came up to me and kicked me in my stomach so hard that I fell to the ground and started to roll down the ravine.

I was badly hurt by the fall, but I stood up and told him he could kill me, but I would not pay him anything. That made him even more angry. He pulled out a big knife he had with him and started running towards me. He tried to stab me, but I moved in time and his knife only ripped my clothes. The other guy came, grabbed hold of him and said I should have listened to them. "Now you are staying here until the police come and get you guys. They will deport you to Afghanistan." We were all scared. Some in our group started pulling out some of their hidden money and gave it to them. But I and a couple of others refused to pay any money. This was only the first day and if we paid these men, other smugglers would keep asking us to pay more and we would run out of money before we reached Istanbul.

After they left, some of our guys came up to me and told me how brave I was. I started to feel proud myself and realized I was making more friends. I saw that people were now listening to me more than ahmad. He was not happy about that, but he was right. I should not have fought with these men. He had more experience than me and knew they could have killed me without any problem. No one

17

was around to question them. I was still inside of Iran and the government would not care if I lived or died. I was only an unwanted refugee in their country anyway.

After about one hour, another group of refugees joined us. I could not believe my eyes when I saw one woman had a small baby in her backpack. I thought, "Wow, Oh my God. How can a woman come to this point and put her life and the life of her newborn child in such danger?" Finally, the two guys came back and asked us to get ready to move on. We were happy to get moving again. We were about to get our first lesson that we should stay together, or we cannot survive. We walked all night and into the next morning before we arrived at another valley. We were tired and exhausted from hiking the mountain trail. I was used to walking, but not on a mountain, and in the dark. My feet were hurting, and I needed some place just to sleep and take off my shoes and thick socks. I had a plastic bag over my socks to protect my feet from moisture. Our shoes would get wet from the melting snow so, we had to wear plastic on top of the socks to keep our socks and feet from getting cold and wet.

We reached a safe place where we could rest for the day until the next nightfall when we would have to start walking again. In the middle of the day, two men came and said that the lady had to leave the group and go with them. Her husband was there. He was a small, innocent young man, unable to stand up to the menacing smugglers. As soon as his wife heard she would have the leave her husband, she started crying. We were all suspicious of these men and what was going on. Why did they ask the lady to go with them? But we did not have any choice but to trust them. In the end, the husband took his wife aside and start talking to her. We could see from the fear in their eyes what they were thinking and what they must have been afraid of, but there was no other option. Her husband kept quiet as she left with the men.

The night was coming, and we knew we would be leaving that place soon. Another smuggler came to guide us, riding a horse. He said we should follow him until the next morning. As we walked, we saw more and more people coming to join us. Most of them were from Pakistan, which made ahmad very happy because he could make them dance to his tune. The smugglers had a hard time communicating with the Pakistanis, but he knew a little of the Turkish language of the smugglers and was fluent in the Urdu tongue spoken by the Pakistanis. There was now a long line of refugees, but everyone walked quietly, following the footsteps of the person in front of them. Glacial ice was everywhere, and it was getting hard to walk. We had to concentrate on walking without slipping. There were a couple of people in the group who were totally unprepared for this trek; they had no shoes and warm clothing. Hiking a mountain trail without proper shoes and warm clothing must have been extremely hard for them, but they kept up with the rest of us through the night.

Walking in darkness gives you a different feeling; it forces you keep your thinking cap on and press forward because there is no other option. As we slowly and carefully walked along the trail, I was thinking that we were all racing minute by minute from the past into an unknown future through treacherous terrains. Any of one of us could die of exhaustion or exposure, or we could slip and fall down the mountain and nobody would find us. We did not choose this hardship, but with every step on the icy path, I was only thinking about the past that was disappearing behind me. I pressed onward with confidence and determination, telling myself I must go all the way to the end.

Suddenly, the stillness of the night was pierced with the screaming sounds of one of the refugees behind me. Just as I had feared might happen to one of us, he slipped on the ice and fell off the side of the mountain. We could hear his voice echoing down and down into the darkness below until the stillness of the night returned. Even if it were possible, no one would go chasing after him to try to find him and rescue him. I wished I could have helped him, but I knew if I tried, I would only put myself in danger and could easily lose my way back to the line of refugees trekking relentlessly through the night. Each of us felt we were responsible for our own life now and no one else's. The night temperatures were so freezing cold that most of those who came with no gloves lost all feeling in their hands. Their fingertips were frozen, and some lost a nail on one of their fingers. Those without proper clothes were crying and saying they could not walk any farther. I didn't understand why they came with no clothes and shoes or any food for the journey. Had nobody told them? I was in the front of the line and ahmad was the last person in the line. Sometimes I looked back and I could see him looking at his feet. He was thinking about the cold too.

We were all very tired when, finally, the guide told us we could sit down and rest quietly for a while. Some of us slept on the ice, and some of us did not know what to do, or how we could rest while exposed to the freezing night air. A few of the guys started smoking a cigarette, but Yunus ran to them and told them to put out the cigarette. He explained that the police could see us from a distance every time they sucked on the cigarette and it lit up. It was not long before we started walking again. We continued through the night until it was almost morning. We arrived at the fence that I thought must have been the border between Iran and Turkey. It was still dark, but because of the radar we were not supposed to pass over the top. They dug some holes under the barbed wire fence so we could squeeze ourselves through and pass under it. Once on the other side, we faced another challenge: a ten-foot barrier that we had to jump down. The first person who jumped down, broke his leg. It was so dark that we could not see where we were jumping. We were not allowed to turn on any light or use a cellphone to see what was below as we jumped. But we had no other way, but to jump and try not to get hurt. Some of us tore our clothes, and some of us landed on the ground with bumps and scrapes. We were all cold, sore, and tired, but we had successfully passed through this last challenge before leaving Iran. I had finished another day of our journey without any great harm.

CHAPTER THREE

JOURNEY OF LIFE AND DEATH.

By the time Our group reached another area that was covered by heavy snow. The snow was both good and bad news for us. The good news was we could eat the snow to quench our thirst and rehydrate our bodies. The bad news was the heavy snow made our walk much more difficult. I remembered when I was back in Afghanistan and how the heavy snow would make it difficult to go out of our home. We could not travel very far because it was too hard to move through the deep snow. When our group reached the top of the snowy mountain, we discovered we could use the snow to slide all the way down to the bottom of the other side. So, thanks to the snow, we could enjoy at least a few moments of our journey.

When it was dawn again, we could see all around us. The guide told us that we were safely inside of Turkey. I was feeling much different now because with every breath, I felt like I was taking freedom into my lungs. I wanted to take a deep breath and take in as much free air as my lungs could hold. I was happy that we had passed the border of Iran without much of a problem. I knew we lost a couple of people, but it could have been much worse. If we were caught by the police, the punishment would have been much harsher than any of the pain and suffering we experienced on the trail out of Iran.

They divided our large party into three groups. Each group had about forty people, and each group had their own guides. For some reason unknown to me, each group departed in a different direction. We walked couple of hours and arrived at a point between two mountains. Our guides told us we should stay there that night and they would come back and pick us up in a car. We were so happy to hear that we did not need to walk any more. We were all very tired that night and were looking for a place to rest and sleep, but there was no good place to lay down to rest. It was bitter cold, and the hard ground was covered with ice and stones everywhere. There were no blankets or hot food for us. We just had to stay awake and wait. We were afraid of what would happen to us if we fell asleep on open ground, exposed to the bitter cold night.

After hours of sitting and wrestling with the freezing cold temperatures, we finally we saw a small closed-body truck coming toward us. We were happy and excited to finally get into a vehicle and make some progress on the trip without walking. I thought I could take off my shoes and sit in a nice warm place for a while. I did not imagine something so simple would one day become my dream, or that my simple dream of riding instead of walking would turn into a nightmare.

The car stopped close to us and they opened the back door. We all ran into the back of the truck without paying attention to where we were going or what we were doing. After a few minutes in the back of the truck (we were almost forty men), we realized that we were inside a refrigerator truck designed to transport meat and food for a company. We were all standing and started to realize that we could not breathe properly. There is no way for enough air to get inside the refrigeration box we were in. All sides were perfectly sealed except for just a small vent that was not big enough to fill the lungs of forty men. The truck was designed for transporting food, not for transporting living, breathing men.

We could feel the truck picking up speed, but we did not know how long we were going to have to stay in that box. We knew we could not survive long without air to breathe. We were lucky the refrigerator was off but the weather outside was cold enough to freeze all of us anyway. Inside the truck it was getting hotter from all the bodies being pressed together. It was becoming increasingly hard to take each breath.it remind me the Nazis killed the milion people with almsot same method,flesh to flesh eye ball to eye ball, We were all getting very angry for the way they had deceived us. We did not know that we were going into another situation that would be worse than walking outside. We started to panic and began hitting the walls of the box to warn the driver that we were dying in the back of his truck. But all the time we were banging on the walls, the driver was only pressing on the gas pedal harder and harder. I believed they must have been aware of the problem. This was not the first time they were doing this. But they were ignoring us.

Some of the guys pulled their knives and tried to poke holes into the metal wall of the car. But those walls were thicker and stronger than expected. All their efforts were unsuccessful. It was getting too hot for us and we had to take off our winter clothes and jackets. That made breathing harder because it started stinking of human sweat and body odors – like the room I entered the first night of my journey. But we were beyond caring; we were dealing with life and death in the back of that truck. Three or four people started to have severe breathing problems, but there was no way to help them. We had a little water and just poured some on their faces hoping it would help. Some of the men started crying, some started praying, and others started cursing. But I told all of them that if they did not stop talking, they would only waste a lot of more the precious little air we had inside. We should all just shut up and be quiet. Yelling and screaming was not going to work. Two of those guys almost died. They were frothing from their mouth and their bodies were twitching like they were having epileptic fits. It was very hard for us to watch this and not be able to do anything the help them.

At last, I could feel the car slowing down and they came to a stopping point. As soon as they opened the door, we all jumped out of the back of the truck. I felt like I had been under water and somebody held my head down to try to drown me. As soon as I could pull my head out of the door, I opened my mouth as wide as I could to take fresh air deep into my lungs. The minute we got out of the truck, the smuggler who opened the door started to run from us to quickly get into the cab of the truck and speed away. They knew we were angry enough to kill them. In fact, one of men in our group was yelling that he would kill them, but we could not catch them. We had lost almost all our strength and could not move our bodies very much. After they sped away and we all caught our breath, we realized that in our desperation to get out of the back of the truck, we had forgotten to grab our things and take them with us. Our last few possessions, except for the clothes on our backs were gone. I completely broke down at that moment and started to cry and scream. I was asking myself what was going on and why do bad things keep happening to us. But there was no answer. Our only option was to deal with it. I was too cold to think, and I felt my blood pressure was dropping fast. I felt tired and sleepy. But just then another guy approached us and told us we needed to follow him.

I was angry but I could not yell or even talk to him. I was so desperate and needy. I felt my heart was breaking like the ice under my feet. I could no longer feel my legs, fingers and lips. I was thirstier and hungrier than I had ever been in my life. More than anything, I needed a warm place to rest and some sleep. I was so dog-tired that I could not walk any more. I was begging for some help from our guide, but all he could say was, "Follow me I'll take you to a warm place." So, we kept walking until we approached a village. I could hear dogs barking and coming toward us, but I didn't care about anything at that point. I felt like anything that could happen to me right then could not be worse than the situation I was already in.

Our guide finally led us to an empty sheep pen. The strong stench of sheep and goats were all around us as soon as we stepped inside. It looked like they just moved the livestock out to accommodate our arrival. Still, it seemed like paradise for us after being exposed to the bitter cold on the mountain trail and then our terrible ordeal inside the meat truck. I could finally find a warm place to sleep – even though it was only on a mound of sheep fodder. I quickly fell into a deep asleep. I never imagined that one day fodder would become a welcome bed and blanket for me. A couple of hours later, our guide came back and asked us to give him money to buy us some food. We were too tired and hungry to negotiate a price with him and just paid the amount he requested. A short time later, he brought us some yogurt with bread; we were disappointed that the meal was so meagre, but there was no other option for us. All we could do was eat without complaining, because this was the first warm, solid food we had to eat after almost a week. All of us got around the big pot and started eating with shaky and weak hands.

After a couple more hours of good rest, two more smugglers came and told us to be prepared to leave. They gave me to wear some old, torn clothes left by other refugees. I was happy to have them because they were at least enough to keep me warm. Slowly, we started walking once again. I felt like I had been hit by a big car and was still not recovered from it. I had lost sensation in some parts of my body. We had to pass along a river, and one of our guides told us, "If you fall into the river no one can help you and you will drown or die in the cold water; just be careful." At one point, we had to cross over to the other side of the river. There were some big stones on the riverbank and more in the river that we could use as steppingstones to get to the other side. The first person who jumped, slipped, fell into the rushing water, and was swept away in a split second. We just saw his two hands and his head bobbing up from under the water, as he cried out for help. But all any of us could do was just look at him; there was no way any of us could be of any help to him. His friends ran after him along the side of the river, but after a couple of minutes they all came back crying, saying, "He just got married. How can we tell his wife, mom, and dad where to go and find him? How hard it will be for them to just have a picture, and not see him anymore." We could not waste mourning the loss of one on our company; seeing others die in front of our eyes had become a daily routine. Now, we had to find a way out to get to the other side of the river. I jumped successfully, and so did another guy. We both stood on top of stones in the river and started helping others to get to the other side. This plan worked very well, and without much problem we could finally help everyone reach the other side of the river to safety.

It seemed like we were getting close to another village. We could hear a cock crowing and dogs barking. In every village we passed through, we realized that their dress and culture was different. Some of the children started running towards us and began talking with the guide. Some of them looked at us like we were freaks. I knew that we were the ones who were weird and different there, but I am sure this was not the first time they saw foreigners trekking through their village. They must have seen many other immigrants before. It was getting about time to stop and rest again. I was ready to go visit another sheep pen for a good recharging nap, but this time, they surprised us and let us into their house. "Oh my God!" I thought. I could not believe it. They had a fireplace that we could sleep in front of. I laid down in front of that fireplace and it was the biggest blessing for all of us. My feet had lost all sensation. I wanted to throw my legs into fire until my legs and feet could feel the sensation of heat once more. I enjoyed the noise of burning coals and crackling wood releasing energy and warming us with their red and blue flames. We spent a couple minutes as close to the fire as we could – until the sensation in our feet and hands were restored. As we sat and warmed ourselves, a woman brought a big pot with food to our room. We were expecting another simple meal of yogurt. But this was another surprise. She had made warm food with meat for us. Our eyes became soaked with tears. We could not believe that we could eat meat hereinside kurdish family,they were so welcoming and kind to us. She also made nice fresh bread for us that smelled so good; it was unbelievable. Not only did they give us a hearty meal, but they did not ask us for any money. But we told each other we needed to pay money to this woman because of their kindness.

A few minutes after we finished eating, one of our guides came and called some of the Pakistani men to step outside. As soon as they did, they started screaming and crying. We were wondering what was going on and stepped outside to see. We could not believe what we saw. The body of the person who fell into the river and was swept away, was found and brought there wrapped in a blanket. I could not look at him. My knees shook, and I sat down and started crying too. We hugged each other. His frozen body had turned into an iceberg; I could see his eyes and they looked like they were asking for help or looking with a hope to be rescued, but he died with eyes open. I wondered if this drama of being refugees would ever come to an end. We went back inside while the Pakistani guys searched for a place to bury their friend.

After a while someone knocked on the door and when the door was opened, we saw the lady and her baby that had been separated from us days before walk in. She was well and happy, crying for joy to be reunited with her husband. They went to another room to talk.

And all thanked God to see the woman and the baby back safe and reunited with her husband. We stayed in that house and rested for a whole day. The fireplace felt very good. Its warmth restored our strength and we felt we would live and keep on going. We needed the energy the fire gave us. The sounds of the crackling wood as it burned was really a peaceful melody to me; it was like someone telling me a story to put me to sleep.

CHAPTER FOUR

ENDLESS ROUT.

We were very close to Van, one of the major towns in Turkey near the border with Iran. All immigrants must pass through this city to go to western side of the country that borders Europe. As soon as it got dark outside, we were ready to move again. Our guide arrived on a horseback and called us out as always. He explained every rule we should follow on this next part of our journey. He cautioned us that there were more police stations along this part of our route, so we should tread very carefully without talking or coughing. He told us that if he gives us the signal, we should run. We all said we understood and agreed to follow his instructions.

We were keeping up with the guide as best we could, but because he was riding a horse, sometimes the pace was just too fast, and we had to struggle to catch up with him. At times we were gasping for breath but had to keep pressing on at the same fast pace. As we walked, we could see the stuff other refugees left on the road: back packs, bags, clothes and water bottles. The rusted and mangled metal objects discarded along the way indicated that the route we were traveling must have been used by smugglers for a long time. I saw some stones on the way that were painted red or yellow. ahmad told me if you see red color, they are land mines, and you need to be careful not to step on them. It was scary for me; one small mistake could cost my life. A bad injury in the middle of this deserted valley with no hospital or doctor would be fatal. All of us had to be acutely aware of the warnings and danger laying just below the surface of the ground we were walking upon.

After four or five hours of walking, we could see lights approaching us from a distance. I quickly realized they were the headlights of the cars moving up the road toward us. I never imagined I would miss this image of cars and lights. As they came close, a minivan with no windows stopped right in front of us. The driver was a woman and motioned us to get into the car. As soon as we were in, it took off. She was driving as fast as she could; it felt like we were flying down the road. Because there were no seats in the van, all we could do was try to stick to the floor and try not to move.

After spending a couple of days with these smugglers, we could easily identify who was the boss of each crew. Whoever has a couple of cell phones is the boss. The guy that was sitting next to the driver was constantly receiving phone calls and was updating us about the road that we are on. After some time, we reached a big house where they dropped all of us into the front yard. They escorted us inside and led us to a big room. I could smell the same human odors that I smelled in that small house on border, in the back of the crowded truck, and at other points on our journey. I could tell that a big crowd of immigrants were recently removed from this room. It was very dirty, but by this time nothing bothered me; I felt I could sleep anywhere. I could tolerate any conditions or eat and drink anything that wasnot moving. I used to consider myself a picky person, but I learnt differently on this journey. Anything can be a blessing to you when you have lost everything but the will to survive.

They told us it was okay for us to use our cell phones for the moment. We could call our family and let them know we were safe and where we were. We were able to order sim cards, and those in our group that had a phone were happy to share the exorbitant cost of communicating with family members back home. We helped each other so that everyone could call and talk with their family. When I was able to make my phone call, my mom picked up the phone. As soon as she heard my voice she started screaming and crying. She was thanking God that we could talk. The first question she asked me was "Are you ok?" I said, "Yes, mom. No worries. I am ok. No problems." I could not bring myself to say a word about the tragedies and the dramas we had just gone through, and closed my call saying, "Yes, mom. Thank God, I'm okay." I hung up the phone and let others call their families.

It must be stressful, waiting until your child calls you to let you know they are okay. But I wondered, what about the family of the men who did not survive the journey? The man who fell to his death and the man who drowned in the icy river were gone, but somebody back home was waiting to receive their calls. They were waiting for someone to tell them that he was alive and well. But there was nobody to call them. Nobody wanted to tell them, "Your loved one, your son, your precious child did not survive his mom and dad. He is gone. I am so sorry."

I could hear sounds of joy and happiness on the phone. Everyone was crying, but not saying a word about what had passed since they left home. They spoke of their hopes for the future. They talked about their destination – where they wanted to end up – England, France, Italy, etc. All of us were looking forward to some new place that we could call home. Where we would no longer be called immigrants, but citizens.i had one more hope and it was to see my frind again.

After the calls, we sat down for some time, and thought about how the challenges were different now. We were almost eighty people and there was just one bathroom. Besides there was not enough water or toilet paper. Most of us were sick from the things we ate on the way and were not feeling very well. Then some started fighting in the line for the bathroom. Within few minutes the line ended up being a fight between two countries: Afghanistan and Pakistan. We divided into two nationalities. And because most of us were from Afghanistan, we could win and get the bathroom. But was it worth the fight? I was looking at our group and how we were protecting the bathroom door like it was our property. I wondered why we could not sit down and discuss how to share. But I must confess that I was one those people who started the fight and supported the idea of taking control of the bathroom. Sometimes we are so obsessed by the ideology of the group that without being rational, we join them for reasons we don't understand.

We stayed there for two days, which was enough time to get our energy back. We could order any food we wanted, but, of course, we had to pay for it. We learned the concept of "no free stuff" here. The owner of the house came and told us we should be prepared to go in a big trailer to Istanbul. It would be a journey of almost 35 hours. I heard a story about this part of the journey before. It is really exhausting. We would all have to sit for 35 hours in the back of the big truck. You cannot move. You can't use a bathroom. You cannot go out and stretch or even stand up. But, once again, there was no other option. We had to accept it and go on.

One of the guys in our group said, that his friend had jumped out of the truck because he could not control himself for so many hours, sitting in the same place. As soon as he jumped out, another car hit him, and he died instantly. Another guy was saying that some of his friends almost died because they did not have food for three days. The owner came and said. "Be ready in fifteen minutes to move out." We were all suddenly in panic and scared by the all stories we had heard. But we had to go. Instead of thinking about what might be ahead of us, we looked at each other encouraged each other out loud. We reminded each other of all we had overcome so far and said we will overcome this challenge as well. "We are Afghans," we said, "we are born warriors." We must face this problem with courage and not be afraid. After this conversation, everyone was ready to jump into the truck when it arrived.

Some in our group opened the Quran and started reading it and praying. When we were going out of the room one person held the Quran up so we could pass underneath it. This is one of the Muslim beliefs – that the Quran will protect you when you go travelling. So, it will protect you by passing under it or by carrying it in your pocket.

The same mini-van that brought us to this house, came and picked us up. We rode for almost one hour until reached the point where we were transferred into the big truck. There was a big slope and we had to go down to the end of it and wait there for the truck to come. We had to wait for almost twenty minutes for more immigrants to join us. It was not long before our ranks had swelled to one hundred and twenty souls. Every time another person arrived my heart would pound faster. It seemed that everyone felt the same. We all knew the truck was not going to be big enough, but we would have to find a way to squeeze into it anyway.

A truck finally came and stopped close to us. The driver stepped out of the front, walked to the back door, and opened it for us. When he asked us to get in, we all started running into the back of the truck. We knew if we hesitated, we would not find good place to sit. The best places were close to the wall; that way we could lean against the wall for support. We could tell by the smell, that the truck had been used to transport cows and sheep. The walls were short and with every movement you could feel the dirt left by the sheep. I found a place close to the wall and sat down immediately. I had to pull my knees close to my chest so others could sit too. At first, I thought it was going to be very hard for us. I could not breathe, and after we sat down, they covered the truck with some srot of thick cloth so there was no way we could stand up and no one can see us. When the truck started moving, we discovered a good thing: the wind blowing under the tarp that covered us gave us some fresh air to breathe. After an hour's drive, the truck broke down in the middle of the road. The driver came to us and told us if any of us moved when the mechanic got there, we would all go to jail and be deported.

So, we would all have to just sit there and be quiet. We all just bowed our heads on our knees and forced ourselves not to talk.

After the vehicle was fixed, we were back on the road again. The driver gave us couple of boxes of water and asked me and ahmad to give one each to everyone. The temperature was already very hot, and we still had thirty two hours more to go in this truck.and that was the last time he gave us water, we had drink our own pee so we can survive. Every time the car hit a bump in the road, I could feel the cold iron of the car body punch me in the back. The truck was packed way beyond its capacity. So, I had no way to shift my position. I just had to take it. I think normally, if you wanted to transfer humans with this truck, it should not hold more than fifty or sixty people, but we were one hundred and twenty, including a woman and her small child, some personal items, and some back packs. all of us caried knife and start poking hole into cover so we can see alittile bit of outside.

The way we had to sit put too much pressure on our knees. We had to fold them and could not stretch. I was so tired that I fell sleep anyway, but after a while I was awake in the middle of the night. After the sun went down, the weather got cold, but we kept on moving through the night. One of our friends discovered a way to sleep. Three or four of them stretched their limbs in such a way that one person could sleep for at least a few minutes. By working together, they could stretch their arms and legs for a moment and then reposition them to allow the next person in the group to sleep. I tried it too and liked it. It was a short time, but at least I could move my hands, legs, and back freely for a few minutes. One thing I will never forget was having to be in the back of that truck for so many hours with no bathroom. One hundred and twenty people were jammed together, and we had no toilet.

We had to use our same water bottle we had drank from and pee into it. It was a very hard time, but I learned a lot about patience and endurance from this journey.

CHAPTER FIVE

BECOME A HUMAN SMUGGLER

After more than thirty five hours on the road, we could finally hear the cries of sea gulls in the distance; it was an indication that we were close to the sea and that meant we are getting closer to Istanbul and the European side of Turkey. We got even more excited as we caught a glimpse of a bridge overhead because it meant our big dream to see Istanbul was about to come true.

After an hour's drive through the outskirts of Istanbul, the truck pulled into a big yard of a house, stopped, and turned off the engine. We counted every second until we could jump out of the back of the truck. After almost two days and nights we wondered if we could still walk. When they opened the gate and we jumped out of the truck our fears were realized. We quickly discovered that the muscles and joints in our legs were locked up, and we started falling on top of each other. It was very hard for us to stand up and walk at first. It took me about ten minutes to take my first steps. We found a place to lay down under the trees in the yard and stretched out our aching bodies on the ground.

After few minutes some minivans came inside the farm and asked us to get into them. Although the vehicles were smaller, it was just a repeat of we had just experienced –no windows, same smells etc. I don't know about others, but I was extremely irritated and exhausted by this time. I was not able to walk, talk, or even to eat something. I thought to myself, if police came to arrest us and send us back, I would not do anything to resist. The vehicle was driving very fast and I could see the driver talking on the phone. I could see fear in his eyes and face. He was constantly looking around and watching for any suspicious activity around the neighborhoods we were passing through. Others in the back of the minivan must have been as tired and irritated as I was because it was not long before they started arguing with each other. In no time a couple of fights broke out inside the car because of the frustration and the hard conditions we were in. At last, they dropped us off and moved us into the basement of an apartment. I thought this must be the last car we had to ride in for a while. The place where we were had red carpet, a kitchen, and several bathrooms. I thought maybe I can take a shower. I knew I must have been stinking like sheep after almost a week staying in stables and barns and other places where farm animals had been.

After a few hours of rest, we started talking with each other. All of us wanted to have a chance to go and visit Istanbul. We heard a lot about this beautiful city with twenty million population and a beautiful blend of Asian and European cultures. But we could not go anywhere yet. For the time being, it would have to remain a dream. We were informed that it was too dangerous and not worth the risk of being caught to go out right away.

And after all the challenges and difficulties that we had already faced in order to get to this point of our journey, we could wait a little longer to see the sites.

We had only been sitting there for about two hours before something unexpected happened. There was a knock at the door and when one of the guys opened the door the police burst inside. We were all were shocked as soon as we saw his face and the uniform. The guy who opened the door called his other friends standing outside. But we could see that the people who brought us here had been caught by police. It looked like this would be the end of our journey. One of the police officers was going on and on saying in a loud voice, "Deport! Deport!" All our dreams were crashing down; the dreams we had for a prosperous future and a good life seemed dead and gone in an instant. After all the struggles – going without food, the long treks through treacherous mountains and rugged valleys in inclement weather and all the suffering – we would have to go back to Afghanistan. My mind was reeling as I thought that all the situations I braved were for nothing. I wished I had never come. My only consoling thought was at least I would not have to sleep in a stable and be hungry or thirsty anymore.

The policemen came up to us and told us sit down and not to move. I knew ahmad was afraid because this was his third time being caught and deported from Turkey. So, his case was worse than ours. I could not control myself and I put my head down on my knee and my eyes got wet. I was angry with God and wondered again "Why me? Why us?" I was deep in thought when someone slapped my face. I open my eyes and saw a police officer standing in front of me. He asked my name and where I came from. I told him my name and I came from Afghanistan. He took my hand and said, "We are brothers." Then he asked all those from Afghanistan to move to the other room. One of the chief police officers came to me and told me to tell my friends to stay there, and he would come back in a few minutes. Until then we were not to walk out of the room. I told him I understood, and he left us alone in the room. Another policeman came in and asked us if we had any money on us. I told him we had maybe one hundred dollars hidden. He told me to go and tell your friends if you pay one hundred dollars, I will let you go. I asked him if he was serious. I could not believe his offer, but I went inside and told my friends and they agreed to pay the one hundred dollars per person. They gave me all their money, and I went outside and gave it all to that officer. He told us to stay inside for an hour. Then get out and run from there and do not come back.

While we were waiting, we could hear those outside our door, crying and begging for help. Nevertheless, from the sounds they were making, they were being told they were being deported back to where they came from. After almost forty minutes of heart-pounding suspense, it was silent again. We knew we could not stay inside much longer, but we did not know if that policeman was honest or if he was trying to trick us. Maybe this was only a way for the police to know how much money we had. We did not know who else could hiding inside that house. After the hour had passed, we came out of hiding and looked for a way to run. Nobody was in the house; we searched every room, even the bathroom and kitchen, nobody was left inside.

I took advantage of the moment to use the bathroom with no stress of someone standing outside and knocking on the door.

The police had left with the other immigrants and we were free now. I could not believe that as soon as I got out of the building, I could breathe! I felt like a bird. I thought I could fly. I was free and I could go and visit Istanbul. I could go wherever I wanted. As I was still feeling the excitement of my liberation, I heard someone call my name. I looked around and saw ahmad inside a taxi. He was calling me to come on and get in with him. I quickly jumped into the taxi and we started moving, but I did not know where to. ahmad told me he had some friends in Istanbul and we could go to their house. When we arrived at a crowded, bustling street in the middle of Istanbul, we got out of the taxi and started walking. I was very fascinated by everything around me. I could not believe that I was seeing Istanbul with my own eyes. But there I was, walking down the streets of Istanbul.

After a while, someone approached us and introduced himself. His name was Reza; he was one of ahmad's friends in Istanbul. He told us to follow him and don't look around; if we saw any police don't stop or run, just walk normally until we reached his house. As soon as we entered it, I saw that was not his personal house. I could smell the same odors from inside that I had smelled coming from other refugee stops I had made on the road to Istanbul. They had covered over the windows with blankets; the lights were off, and you could not hear a sound from the inside. I was thinking that nobody lived there until I entered the place and saw almost sixty men and children living there.

All of them were sitting down and talking very softly. I asked Reza how long they had been staying here he said, almost five months.

There was no place to walk and sit inside the room. Reza introduced us as smugglers, and after that they brought us tea and cookies. They asked questions, about when we would be sending them out from there. I realized they were on a waiting list of some kind for their destination of London. I thought it quite amazing that some of them were thinking that London is a country. And they were telling me they were on their way to the country of London. I did not know what I was supposed to say, but talked as if I knew what was happening, "Okay. we will do it as soon as we can."

I started making friends with one of the immigrants named Ali. He came there from Pakistan, but he was originally from Afghanistan. He told me his family was rich, and he was going to London to study there. He finished TOEFL (Test of English as a Foreign Language) and his English was very good. Later I started talking with two other immigrants named Salim and Hyder. They were brothers and both had the same hefty build. They told me they were on their way to London to play cricket. They were professional cricket players at home but wanted to find better opportunities to play in England and make their fortune.

I asked Reza, if he could take me to the beach. I wanted to see the sea. I had never seen a beach in my life and thought it would be fun. Reza took us to the beach that night. And that night he started telling me the routes we needed to use to go and come. He was teaching me all the tricks of the trade he used for survival, because he was illegal too. Reza did not even have an ID for himself. While we were returning from the beach, he asked me where I came from, why I was there, and where was I going. I told him I wanted to go to work. I loved sports, including boxing and football. But my passion was to find a good place to live and call it home; to make lots of money in order to make my family happy. That was the primary reason for my travel and bearing with all these problems. When we came back to the house, I was able to talk to my mom for the first time since I arrived in Istanbul.

That night, I could sleep well after talking with my mom and telling her of my recent adventures.

Early in the morning Reza woke me up to go and get breakfast for everyone. I could not believe it, but he bought 140 pieces of bread just for breakfast. The bakery that supplied it was making bread just for him. They were not selling bread to anybody else, just to Reza. They were consuming almost 1,000 units of bread per day for breakfast, lunch, and dinner. Soon I was being his helper – not just for bread, but for all the markets around that area that were suppliers for Reza. He was purchasing everything for the immigrants: fruit, chicken, vegetables, etc. Reza told me he made almost $120 dollars per day by purchasing everything for less and upping the charges for all of it to the immigrants because it was too risky for them to go out and purchase anything for themselves.

CHAPTER SIX

TASTE OF MONEY

One day, ahmad told me he was going to work. I asked him, "Work? What is your job?" He laughed and said, "Smuggling humans, of course." I was shocked and asked him "Do you do the same job?" He told me there was no option because they don't give immigrants jobs in Istanbul; they are here illegally. So, this is the best job you can find, and you will get paid more than anyone.

A little later, Reza brought me his phone and told me his boss wanted to talk to me. I took the phone, and the man on the other end introduced himself. His name was karim too, but he was known as "Dark karim." I remembered him from a few years before when my uncle was in Istanbul. At that time "Dark karim" was showcasing himself and his power. He was the biggest mafia man for human trafficking in Turkey. His ability to transfer humans started from Karachi, Pakistan and went all the way to England. He transferred them by ship, taxi, and bus. I was shocked that he wanted to talk to me. He said he had another home like this one Reza was managing and he needed some brave guy to manage it for him. He said he did not pay any salary, but I would be free to find the way to make money from them any way I wanted. He said I could sell them phones, buy them food, and charge them extra. Or I could take them outside on a tour and charge them for going out like his other smugglers. I knew then why I had to pay money to the smugglers on border; they don't get paid and this was the only way they make money. They just find a way to get their money from the refugees – with force or without it – but they needed to make money. After he explained every benefit, I agreed. I knew that I did not have enough money to go to England. So, I would work for "Dark karim" for a few months and then I would have enough money to go from what I made here. We struck the deal and the next morning Reza took me to the place I

58

would be managing. It was another house like the others – same unsanitary conditions and smells. It looked all too familiar and was what I was expecting. What was different was the people in this house did not care about me and did not pay attention to me when I arrived. I believed that because they had stayed there without anybody controlling them, and they had learned how to go outside on their own, they realized there was nothing to be scared about.

When I introduced myself, they did not respect me at all. They did not make any tea for me, which in our culture is the most basic act of hospitality and respect. I was upset and felt afraid that I would not be able to control these people. They felt they knew everything, I knew myself. Before I got there, ahmad warned me that I would need to do something dramatic to scare everyone in that room before they would start obeying and listening to me.

He told me from the first moment I walked into that room, they must think they need me and that I am in charge, or they won't ever listen to me.

After a few minutes of being ignored, I said, "Okay, you guys need some punishment!" I knew they were all strict Muslims and they don't drink alcohol. Muslims won't drink because they think it is a sin and if they sin, their God will punish them and send them back to their country. So, I walked out of the room and went to a market where I purchased two beers. When I came back inside, I turned to others and told them, "All of you guys should listen to me." I found a place to sit and started drinking the beers. They were all shocked by my actions and started whispering into each other's ears and talking about me. I knew something bad was about to happen and if I could not immediately get control of this house, I needed to quit this job. I had to prove myself.

After couple minutes, one of the men who had a long beard shouted at me, "Hazara! Infidel!" The Hazaras are a hated ethnic group from Afghanistan. As soon as he said that, I found the long metal shaft from the other room and attacked him very badly. As I was beating and choking him, I told him to look into my eyes and asked him if he saw any fear in them. I said, "Yes, I am an infidel!" And he told me, "You are not scared, not even of God." I released him, and nobody came close to me. I was acting like a drunk person and they were all scared of me. One of the big guys came up to me and asked me to please let him go. I told them that nobody could go outside anymore without my permission. From then on, everyone would have to ask me. I made it clear to them that I was the one who was responsible for that house after that time. All of them without question said, "Okay. Okay, sir." I threw way the staff and went outside to walk a few minutes and calm myself down.

After I came back, everything was different. Their behavior towards me changed totally. They were listening carefully to whatever I said and were respecting me. I understood then why ahmad battled with everyone everywhere he was going. He was fighting for a good reason: the refugees would not listen to or obey anyone unless they were shown who is boss right away. So, this was another lesson I needed learn, hold on to, and implement in my life. I was determined to practice this method with everybody – even after I got married, I felt this method was going to work. I remembered how I was treated the first day of my journey. Even before I left Iran, when I was still in that valley, they almost killed me with a knife and insulted me because I would not obey them. And now, I was doing the same to others that they had done to me. It was like a chain of command. You waited for your opportunity to move up the chain. And when your opportunity came, you would have your turn to push others around. The top man took advantage of everyone else and made them do what they wanted.

After that night, I immediately started making money. I sold phone calling cards and minutes so they could call their families. Every time money was transferred to them from another country, I would charge a commission for handling their money. I charged them for everything. Besides charging them extra for food, I arranged for a barber to come to the house and give them hair-cuts. If they wanted to go outside to take shower, I would charge them a fee. I charged them extra for everything and for any service I performed for them. Soon, I was making a substantial amount of money running the refugee safe house and was very happy with the way things were going. I started enjoying my life in Istanbul. I was spending money at bars and casinos every night with my friends ahmad and Reza. For the first time, I owned my own phone, and always carried it in my pocket. I had turned into a professional smuggler like the others in no time. My boss gave me all authority to run the house and I was able to control all phone calls in my network from Pakistan all the way to England. I was talking over the phone all day and I found a lot of new friends and connections all around the world. I was involved with human trafficking all around the world and for a price, could make fake passports, visas, and identification papers for anyone who needed them.

One day my boss called me and asked me to go to the "zero point." Zero point was code for the place where we took immigrants by sea in rubber boats to Greece. It was a very hazardous job and a dangerous place, but I said I would do it. I was taught how to check the weather, windspeed, and how to deal with border police. I bought a special lens with night vision so I could see in the dark. They gave me twelve Afghans to smuggle and told me, I was responsible to take them to the zero point and make them ready to send to Greece. My duty was to find the best place to launch the boats and have a couple of connections waiting for them in Greece near any beach where they might land. Then my connections would send the immigrants to the mainland of Greece from there.

My first challenge was no one wanted to sell us bus tickets. I had to make fake police permission papers for them. After I transported them by bus to the place closest to the zero point on its route, I would have to find a taxi driver to take us the next step to a place closer to the beach where we could walk the rest of the way. It took me couple days of searching and planning while sleeping in the bus station at night, but I finally found the guy I was looking for. I offered him a significant amount of money to take us, and he accepted. His name was Halil and he was a brave guy. He was raised in a city near the beach called Ayvalik. It would be two hours by boat from there to the Greek Island of Lesbos. At its closest point, the island was less than five miles from the Turkish coast. Once they reached Lesbos, they would have to make their way to southeast side of the island to the port of Mytilene. Although it was dangerous, this is the best way to send immigrants with minimal risk of being caught.

The first group came, and I picked them up from the bus. Halil and his friend came in two cars and were ready to do their part. We got them into taxi at midnight and started driving toward the beach. It was not easy. It was a very stressful and scary job traveling in the dark, knowing there were a lot of police around. They are always searching for terrorists and illegal immigrants who try to slip past them to get into Greece. Halil had to drive without lights and that made his job harder. But after forty minutes we got to the point I had found on the Google map and he dropped all of us. I paid him his money and he was the happiest person I've ever seen. They quickly disappeared into the night.

After a few seconds, we picked up the boat with the life-jackets and their backpacks and started to carry them. We would still have to climb a couple of rugged hills before we reached the point we wanted. My phone was ringing constantly, but I did not want to answer it. I was trying to be silent. The route reminded me of some of the terrain we traveled through in Iran and eastern Turkey. It was the same story as before, but this trip did not last as long, and we got to the zero point after only an hour's walk.

First, I had to find a place where they could change their clothes and put air in the boats. I made sure all were wearing their life jackets. I made a check of the per kilometer wind speed and used my special night vision camera lens to make sure that no police or anyone else was near us. It only took a few minutes for everyone to get ready to jump into the boats. They hid between the bushes until I gave them the signal that it was safe to put the boats into the water and shove off. It was a different feeling for me, I had done everything for them so that they could escape to a better life. But I was staying there - maybe forever. No one knew for sure what would happen in the next hour or two. Their journey might end with them being arrested by the police; some might pass successfully to where they were hoping to settle; some of them might disappear into the night and never be found again. They had all come to this point, but each had a different story and would have a different destiny. They prayed one last prayer, put their boat into the water, and let them go. I could see them as they drifted around for a few minutes, but they finally got their oars straight and after a few more minutes, they disappeared over the waves.

I had to walk back same way I came until I reached the point where I could call Halil and ask him to come and pick me up. It was scary waiting all alone in the darkness of the middle of the night. All around me I could hear the noises of different animals, but I had to keep walking. This was the life I had chosen, and I believed there was other option for me.

After approximately an hour and a half of walking, I found the main road and called Halil. A short time later he showed up and picked me up. He was totally drunk and messed up, driving like crazy. I could see what extra money was for him; like too many others I encountered in life, the negative influence of money was predictable. However, it did not take long for him to drop me at one of the small hotels in town. I went inside and rented a room. I was able to go to sleep that night with good news from the immigrants I sent; they passed the ocean successfully and made it to the other side to Greece. My first major mission was accomplished! In a very short time this would become the routine for me. The same thing every time – over, and over again. Little did I know that a night was coming when I would have a totally different experience – one that caused me to completely change the course I was on.

CHAPTER SEVEN

SEEKING FREEDOM

I started that fateful night feeling uneasy. Suddenly I realized I was smelling bad and discovered all my clothes and hair were full of lice. That was a really horrifying experience. My whole body was itching, and I could see the lice crawling all over me. After I dropped my latest group at the zero point and saw they were safely gone, I was lost in my thoughts. I started thinking about my life so far. I was feeling homesick and missed my old city, my home and family. I was thinking of the past and worrying about my future. What if I got arrested? If they caught me and put me in jail, what would happen to my mom and dad? What would they think of me? My mind was filled with many questions about where all this was leading me to. After two or three hours of being lost in my thoughts, I realized that I was now lost in the middle of the forest.

I had totally lost my sense of direction, and it seemed like everything around me looked the same. I could not find the main road. All I could see were trees, rocks, and hills. It was impossible for me to find the route back to town in the dark. I called Halil on the phone, but he could not help me. He was drunk again, and how could he know where I was anyway? After a while, I was tired and thought I would sit down and wait until sunrise. A few minutes after I sat down, I heard something behind me. It sounded like someone was walking around behind me. I was using the old 0011 Nokia cellphone common at that time. It was equipped with a flashlight, which made it very popular with the immigrants – it seemed like every one of them had one. When they were not talking on their phone, they would usually be playing the popular Snake Game that came loaded on the phone, which also made it a favorite choice. When I turned on the flashlight, I saw a bear standing in front of me and looking straight at me.

Encountering a bear was the last thing expected and I did not know what to do. I knew I should not run but had no idea of exactly what I should do. I was scared to death, but slowly stepped back, turned off the flashlight, and jumped on the tree next to me. I don't remember how I climbed that tree; I only remember I found myself on the top branches. I hugged the tree as hard as I could. After couple minutes I did not hear anything more from that bear. I did not see him, but I felt he might be hiding somewhere close by.

Unless you have had the same thing happen to you, you cannot know how frightening it is to come face to face with a wild bear. I was terrified at the sight of that bear and imagined him opening his mouth wide and trying to eat me alive! But to my surprise, up there, on the limb of a tall tree, I was able to see the main road. I could see my way out of the forest, but how could I get there?i said mybe god send that bear to scare me and force me to climb a tree.

I called Halil again and told him what was going on, but he could only start laughing at my predicament. This made me more upset, but there was no reason he should believe my crazy story. I could see his car in the distance, coming in my direction. When he was close to the point where I could reach him, I told myself I had to climb down and run as fast as I could to the car. If I did not move then, I would have to wait there until it got dark again. I decided that running was better than waiting there all day in the hot sun. I took another look around and did not see the bear. So, I slowly slid down the tree and after my last cautious step down to the ground, I ran as fast as I could. The branches of bushes and trees were hitting my eyes and face, but I did not care. I could only think that I was trying to save my life and was running toward the safety of Halil's car.

By the time he saw me running towards his moving car, the sun had risen, and it was now early morning. As I approached his car, I could hear gunfire, and when I turned my head in the direction the shots came from, I could see a police car in distance that had been chasing Halil. He said he could not stop, and I had to run and jump through an open rear window that he had rolled down for me. Fortunately, I was able to jump into the moving car and he pressed the gas pedal as hard as he could. When we were far enough ahead of the police car chasing us, Halil turned off the main road and we hid in the jungle until everything settled down. When the police car was long gone, we returned to the city and he dropped me back at my hotel.

It was still early in the morning, when I quietly stepped inside the hotel lobby, but the front desk clerk looked at me suspiciously. I greeted him as I passed by, went straight into my room and locked the door behind me. I took off my clothes and went to bed. I was extremely tired from all the walking, climbing, and running and did not want to be disturbed. So, I turned off my phones and threw them under the bed. I was just about to go to sleep when I heard a knock on my door. I cracked the door open to see who was there and saw the police standing outside. They pushed the door open and forced me to step back and sit down on the couch next to my bed. They asked for my ID. All I had was a paper from the United Nations with my picture on it. While one of them was scrutinizing my ID, and asking me questions, the other policeman was searching inside the room. If they looked under my bed, it would have been all over for me. I had all three of my cellphones with me and all my phone numbers from all around the world were saved on them. Not only that, but all my text messages with Halil and the others in the smuggling network I worked with were on those phones. In my pocket I had almost three thousand dollars cash, and a printed map of the border and night vsion camera in my backpack.

If they searched me and found the large sum of cash in my pocket, they would certainly suspect that I was involved in some kind of illegal activity. They would have torn my room apart looking for evidence to support their suspicions. As it was, they searched my bed, but never looked under it. After a couple of minutes of poking around in my room, So, after apologizing for disturbing me, they left. I quickly closed and locked the door behind them. My heart pounding so hard that I felt it would fly out of my mouth. I could not believe that they never looked in my bag, checked my pockets, or looked under the bed.

After they left, I was in a state of shock. I did not know how they found me or why they came to my room. I fell back down on my bed, but I was too nervous to sleep. It was almost lunchtime when I gathered all my things, put on fresh clothes and threw my lice infested clothes in the trashcan. I told myself that this was a clear warning that I should not stay there anymore. If I stayed there much longer, they were going to come back and arrest me. And if not today, sooner or later, I was going to be caught in the act of human trafficking. I sent a text to my boss and told him I was coming back. I could not stay there anymore. I had been there almost three months and by then everyone – including the police – knew my face and where I was staying.

When I got back to Istanbul, I went straight to ahmad's home. He was renting a very nice house in a luxurious neighborhood in Istanbul. he was making a lot of money then and could afford an expensive house. I had only been staying there with him for two days before my phone started ringing again. I had become a well-known contact for smuggling and once people found out I was back in Istanbul they would not leave me alone. I knew it was time for me to go back to work and start making money again. I was not looking forward to dealing with the headaches and hassles of the work I was doing. For a couple of days, everything was going well.

I was used to having some trouble from the police and being threatened by some of the other smugglers competing with me for the business. I had to be aware of my surroundings and watch every movement around me and my house all the time.

All the stresses and strains on me of the past few months were starting to get to me mentally and emotionally. I was starting to get paranoid and was convinced that one car had been following me all day. ahmad was waiting for me when I got home. When I told him that I was suspicious of one car that seemed to be following me everywhere, he only laughed at me and did not believe me. I felt I like I was being watched all the time. I started wearing a disguise and fake hair to go out the door of my home – even to walk to the outhouse to use the bathroom. I started to have a bad feeling that something terrible was going to happen to me if I stayed in Istanbul. I convinced myself that I had to go back to Iran. I felt strongly that I could not stay where I was any longer. So, I decided to go back and visit my family as soon as possible and rest for a couple of weeks. As soon as I felt better, I would come back.

I purchased my bus ticket and traveled back to Van that same night. It was a totally different experience than my journey from Van to Istanbul. Instead of being packed like sheep in the back of a

stinking truck, I rode inside a bus in relative comfort. It did not take long before I was back in the
same city in Turkey where I arrived when I first
crossed the border from Iran. I got a hotel room and
called one of my friends and asked him if he could
send me back across the border by the same route I
came from. He warned me that it would be a very
dangerous trip for me. I would be going alone, and
no one would be with me to help me. It would just
be me and the guide. I told him I understood and
that it would be okay with me; I needed to get out
of Turkey as soon as possible.

I stayed in the hotel for a couple days and waited for my friend to send his colleague to pick me up
and guide me back to Iran. After leaving the hotel,
he drove me to his house near the border. When we
arrived, and before I entered his house, he took me
to his bathroom and told me to go inside and stay
the night there. I argued with him and asked why I
could not come inside and why I had to stay outside in the bathroom. I asked him, "Do you not
know who I am? I'm the one who is sending all
these immigrants to your house, and you want me
to stay outside overnight in your bathroom?" He
got mad and pushed me inside the bathroom and

closed the door. I was furious over the whole matter, but there was nothing I could do. My phone was not working anymore and there was no way to call my friend and ask him what was going on here. So, I spent the night inside the bathroom. I could not sleep. I could not even sit down. In the morning they brought me some bread and tea to drink. I was not very hungry, but I ate it because there would be no markets and no place to order food for the next few days. For now, I could only eat whatever food was provided for me.

After a few hours, it was midday. A stranger came and started talking with the homeowner as they stood inside in the yard. Through a hole in the door, I could see and hear them from inside the bathroom door. I understood that they were talking about me. After they stopped talking, he opened the door and asked me to follow him. When I went outside the stranger opened the trunk of his car and asked me to get in.

I complied without an argument because I was thinking that anything would be better than staying in that bathroom another night.

When we started to move, I realized that some-one else was sitting in the front seat. The driver kept talking to him in their Kurdish mother tongue. From the little bit I could understand, they were not saying anything of consequence. A short time later, I could smell the smoke of a cigarette that they were smoking inside the car. Then, after almost another half an hour, they stopped the car and removed me from the trunk.

I was in a village that I had never seen before. When I came from Iran, we had not passed this way, so everything was new to me. They took me to the stable and put me inside. Sitting inside was an Afghan family. "Thank God." I thought, now there was someone I could talk with who understood my language. They were waiting there for their fake passports so that they could travel by bus to Istan-bul. I told them they were lucky; I was in the back of a truck for more than 35 hours before reaching Istanbul. Right away, I became friends with that family and gave them my phone number. I told them if they needed any help in Istanbul to let me know and I would see to it that they got the help they need. "But don't look at me now," I said, "I cannot do anything here." I passed the day happily with that family.

Then, after midnight, another young man came and opened the door. After spending hours inside the stable, we had gotten used to the smells, but as soon as he opened the door, he held his nose to keep the harsh odors of farm animals from offending his senses. He told me to get my backpack and come with him. I said good-bye to my new friends and followed him out the door. I was expecting to see a car waiting outside, but only saw a horse standing there. He got on his horse and told me follow him. When I asked him if he expected me to walk when he was riding alone. He turned to me and with stern voice said, "Yes. What did you expect?" He was talking constantly and told me stories about being a smuggler and how Iranian soldiers had opened fire on him. Twice he was wounded in the leg and his father was killed in this way. He went on and on through the night. I walked behind him almost four hours. It was too dark to see, but I knew we were in the mountains near the border of Iran. It was the scariest place I had ever been. Every sound we made echoed from the mountains and the darkness that surrounded us like a thick blanket.

When we reached the top of a mountain that must have been very close to the border, my guide suddenly turned his horse and stopped. He looked at me and told me to keep going until morning. "Just keep going straight, and someone will come and meet you." I was shocked. I told him that he could not just turn and run away, leaving me all alone in the dark on a strange trail where I could easily lose my way. "You're crazy! You can't leave me here alone. If I get lost, who will find me?" He just kept telling me that he could not go any farther with me. It was too dangerous for him. I should just keep going straight ahead. I kept arguing with him. I told him "No. I will come back with you." He insisted that I could not do that and with a kick to the side of his horse, he quickly rode away. I was running after him trying to catch up to him, but he was too fast for me. He disappeared into the darkness, leaving me on the trail to fend for myself.

I was terrified and looked around me and listened, but all was dark and there was no noise. I was afraid that the smallest sound coming from darkness around me might be something that could kill me. I was so scared at that moment that I did not know what to do. If some animal were to attack me, I did not have so much as a small knife to defend myself. I just sat down next to a big rock to hide and thought about what I should do now.

CHAPTER EIGHT

SEE MY MOTHER AGAIN

After a few minutes of being afraid of the dark and worrying about what might happen to me, I realized I had to go on. I simply could not sit there and wait. So, I took a drink of water and told myself this was not the first time in my life that I was all alone in the middle of nowhere. "You have to be strong, i told my self Mehdi. You can do this." I took my first step; my foot was shaking, but the second step was stronger. And with each step I grew more confident that yes, I could make it. I kept telling myself to keep my feet on the ground and press onward. I kept my head down and looked at my shoes as I walked. I was too scared to look around. I started going faster and picked up my pace, telling myself I just had to keep going straight ahead. I walked that way for almost five hours without stopping.

Finally, I saw what looked like a small light flashing in the dark far ahead of me. Soon I realized that someone must have been holding a flashlight, turning it on and off. But who was it? It could be a friend or foe as far as I knew because my guide did not inform me of any signal to light my way to the end of the trail. I was frightened and jumped into a hole near me and waited to see what would happen. Then I heard someone calling my name and I knew this must be the person the guide told me would be waiting for me to take me on the next part of my journey home. I jumped up and ran to where he was standing. When he saw me coming, he told me to come and follow him. I took a deep sigh of relief and thanked God I had made it. I looked behind me and could see the shadow of the mountain I had crossed. I was amazed how I managed pass through the night and make it down that mountain by myself. i proud my self actually.

A couple of minutes later, I saw a couple of horses tied up near a tree. He got up on one of the horses and told me to follow him on foot. I told him how tired I was and begged him to let me ride with him, but like my other guide, he ignored my complaining and made me walk behind him. I had to keep pace with him, even when we crossed a stream. It was not fast or deep, but it made my shoes and pants soaking wet. I was too tired care. I felt like I had no more energy left and could not walk another step when we came to a village. I could hear some people speaking Farsi and I realized that I might be inside Iran, or at least very near it.

This time, my guide took me into his home. He sat me down next to the fireplace and told me I could sleep if I wanted to. He told me he would be back in the afternoon to pick me up. I immediately fell into a deep sleep. I did not realize it was night again until someone came and woke me up. He told me to get ready to leave. I was extremely hungry and ate the last small piece of bread from my backpack. As I was getting ready to leave the room, I felt more stress than before because I knew I was very near the Turkish border. This region is the most dangerous part of the journey, not just because of the human smuggling going on, but because everything being smuggled in and out of Iran and Turkey passes through here. In addition to all the humans being trafficked, Alcohol from Turkey to Iran and gas from Iran to Turkey are two of the other major items being smuggled. And here there are more people on both sides of the border that do these kinds of jobs. Because of the poor economy of this region, and the fact that the government cares very little about these people, they have few options for survival. Their daily lives are marked by hunger and suffering and for many, smuggling is their only real option for making money.

I did not have to wait too long before an old man came and introduced his son to me. He told me that his son would take me to the other side of the border. It was not too far to go now – just a couple more hours of walking. That was acceptable to me, only I hoped it would be the last time I would have to walk on this trip. Because there was a police station situated on top of a mountain overlooking that section of the border, we had to cautiously move around the base of the mountain, hiding ourselves from the searchlight that lit up the entire mountain as it circled around in the night sky. Once we reached the border and stepped inside of Iran, my guide led me to his car and drove me a few miles to the closest village. As soon as he dropped me there, I saw one of the other smugglers I was working with over the phone. He greeted me, but as soon as I started praising him for his help getting me back to Iran, he stopped me and told me instead to thank God I was still alive because most people were not that lucky.

He immediately drove me to the city. It had been a long time since I was able to sit in the front seat. When we reached the bus station, he bought me a ticket for Tehran, the capital of Iran. In another ten hours, I would be home again. I used my friend's phone to call home and let them know I was on the way to see them. As soon as my mother knew I was on the way, she was crying as usual, but this time she was crying tears of joy. I told her to wait and I would be there to give her a hug in the morning. A few minutes later, the engine on bus started making noises and we were moving down the road to the place where my heart was longing to be.

I was so excited that I had to call my friend ahmad and tell him that I was in Iran. He was shocked to hear I was back home. I told him to please be careful because I had a strong feeling that something bad was going on there, but he only laughed at me again. He told me I was still new at the smuggling game and did not know the job as well as he did. I said okay and wished him good luck. Before I hung up the phone, I asked him to take care of my house back in Istanbul until I returned in about a month. It was a bold pronouncement for me. Yes, I had my visa in my pocket, and I was sounding confident that I would be back in Turkey after a month, but who knew what would happen the next time I tried to cross the border into Turkey.

All the way to Tehran, I was too excited to sleep. My dad came and picked me up at the bus station driving his new car. He was so happy to see me, and I was happy to see him again. He was looking and feeling much better than when I last saw him. He looked younger and stronger and was thanking me because of the money I was sending him every month. I was feeling very proud of myself because I bought the car for him with money that I made from smuggling immigrants out of Turkey. My parents had a new house with all new things inside. Before I left Iran, my father was working 18 hours every day just to pay the rent and feed us. Now, for the first time in their lives, my parents were able to own a house and a car.

When the car pulled into the parking lot of our new house, I saw my mom and my sister standing at the door to the house. They jumped from the door and started crying and laughing. They had been waiting for this moment for a long time. Smuggling is not an easy job. I worked hard night and day and put my life in danger to make good money. But I did not regret it because I was doing it all for my family. I was especially happy now because I was able to see with my own eyes how much I had done to make their lives better.

I was seeing them after four years, but it seemed like the time had passed so fast. I could tell that my mother was feeling better too. Now I could see for myself how I had been able to relieve some of the pressures and burdens from my parents' shoulders. We hugged each other again and went inside. Everything was brand new. My mother had everything she had always wished to buy for her house, but they were too poor to have before. I fought off any feelings of superiority I might have. My dad had worked hard and had done the very best he could for us. He had done nothing to be ashamed of. I could take risks he could not take. I crossed the border and made money as a smuggler, but he could never do that because he had wife and children to take care of.

I was not back home long before my mom made my favorite food for me. After I ate, I told her I needed to go buy a SIM card for my phone. She offered me the key to the car, but I did not want to risk driving without a license. It was nice having a personal car, but I did not want to get into trouble while I was home. When I went outside, it was as if nothing had changed. My surroundings were the same as when I left, but I knew I had changed. I came back with a lot of money in my pocket and this time, I could buy whatever I wanted. Just before leaving Turkey, I had made forty thousand dollars from the last boat I sent to Greece. It was a huge amount of money for me. I knew that if I spent my whole life working in Tehran, I could not make that much money.

It did not take long before I gave into the temptation to drive our car even though I did not have a driver's license. I got the key from my father and drove out onto street. I turned the music up loud and was driving fast up and down every street with music blasting from my radio. Everybody was looking at me like I was a crazy young fool, but I wanted people to look at me and see what I could do. Some people in my neighborhood recognized me. No doubt, they were surprised to see me, a poor immigrant from Afghanistan, driving a new car. I was not driving for very long when I realized ahmad was calling me on my phone. To call Iran from Turkey was very expensive, so when I picked up the phone, I told him to hang up and I would call him right back. But he did not wait for me to return his call and he kept calling me. It was then that I realized something must be wrong. I pulled over and stopped the car so I could answer his call and talk to him when my phone rang again. When I heard his voice, it was shaking and sounded scared. He said the police had found the house where we were staying. They were pounding on the door and telling him if he did not open immediately, they would break it down. I told him not to open the door. I was angry with him because I had warned him that something bad was about to happen, but he did not listen to me. He abruptly ended the call and when I tried to call him back, there was no answer. The phone had been turned off.

I did not have any news from news for the month I stayed in Iran. I was worried, but I told my mom that it was time for me to return to Turkey. She did not want me to go, but I told her I had to get back to work and promised I would see her again the next year. I had wasted almost eighteen years of my life in Iran and pleaded with her to let me go. She reluctantly agreed to let me go. I found another person who was involved with human trafficking from Iran to Turkey. His price was higher than I paid before, but he could make me a passport so I would not have to walk all week to cross the border like I did before. We reached an agreement and the deal was struck. The day came for me to say goodbye to my family again.

CHAPTER NINE

BACK TO WORK

When the moment arrived for me to depart for my journey back to Turkey, it was the same farewell scene of many tears and final embraces as was my first time leaving home. The taxi arrived and we made our getaway from Tehran – a place where I never felt I belonged anyway. It was the same travel arrangements as the last time I traveled to the border. We changed from the taxi to a bus that took us as far as the roads would take us inside Iran. I felt no stress and had none of the fear of heading off to an unknown place. This time I was the experienced traveler and served as calming influence for one of my cousins that had decided to make the trip with me. I had promised to take care of him along the way and so I was only worried about his welfare. Another important thing was different about this trip; I had spent a whole month destressing and eating home cooked meals or eating in different restaurants in the city. I had gained almost ten pounds and was not sure I could make it if they asked me to walk long distances over rugged mountain trails like before. In the end, it might be my cousin who had to take care of me instead of the other way around like it was supposed to be.

This was the first time in my life that I had seen my cousin. My family lived in a different city from his. Because his mother was Iranian, I was wondering why he was so anxious to leave. I thought his treatment in Iran would be better than mine. When I asked him, he shook his head and told me it was worse than mine. The government officials told his mother that because she married someone from Afghanistan she would be treated like a foreigner. They would not help her with anything. After hearing his story, I was thinking how we called Europeans "infidels," but they did not treat people that way. In the West, they accept you, give you a place to live, and support you. regardless of your religion or background, they will give you citizenship regardless of your race, tongue, Where I came from, there was only hate and discrimination against anyone that was from a different place. I wondered where this hate and loathing came from. I am Hazara, and Hazar are Shia. I know that 98% of Iranians are Shia, and so, you would think that they would care about us, but they don't. Instead they treat us like nothing. Sometimes I would hear a story about some government official in Iran insulting an Afghan as a way of showing off in front of other Iranians. Iranians were very proud of themselves and often acted like they were better than others. After hearing my cousin's story, I said, "Okay, brother. Let's go. We both have the same problems in Iran."

When we finally reached the point where it was time to walk, I told the guide I would pay him double if I did not have to walk. But he gruffly told me to shut my mouth and walk like the rest of them. Once more, I realized I should not trust any of these people. I should not have been surprised because after all, I had been doing the same thing in Istanbul. I had learned from them how to manage refugees and applied the same techniques to control anyone weaker than I was.

I really struggled this time walking up the mountain. Ill behind the group and if my cousin was not with me, I could have gotten lost. After a few hours of walking we reached the point where we could travel by bus again. We came to the same city I had passed through couple of years before. This time, instead of just passing through, I stopped to have fake passports made for me and my cousin. A man came and took our pictures. When he returned, it was the first time in my life that I held a passport in my hand with my name on it. Although it was not real, it would give me the opportunity to travel without someone else buying tickets for me. Once I started using it, I could not believe the power of this document. Now I had an ID. It was the same thing every refugee is chasing – paperwork, an ID card – anything that allows you to officially use your own name in the country you are in. The Passports allowed us to pass all police stations and checkpoints successfully from that city up to Istanbul. Nobody suspected us and there were no problems for us. We just showed our Passports and they let us through. It seemed amazing to me that I could travel with no stress and not have to walk a week or more to avoid a single police station. It was an indescribable feeling for me. It was like being a newborn

baby and experiencing everything totally new and
fresh.

When we arrived inside the city of Istanbul, I
rented a room for my cousin and me to stay for a
couple of days while I checked out the situation. I
told him I had to go and check my house and see
what had happened to my things. He pleaded with
me not to go there, but I explained to him that I had
a lot of things there, including a laptop and several
important documents that I hid in the kitchen before I left for Tehran. I did not know if they were
still there, but I had to go and check. When I arrived
at my house, I discovered that they had changed the
lock. So, I had to go find a locksmith to open the
door. The locksmith told me that the police called
him there the previous month to open the door. I
asked him what happened, and he told me they arrested the guy they found hiding inside. When they
arrested him, he had a lot of phones and money on
him. The police said he was a smuggler from Pakistan.

I lied to him and told him I had been out of the
country for two months and someone broke into
my apartment. He informed me that he must have
been the person they arrested as he handed me a

new key to the apartment. After he left, I went inside. It looked as if the place was hit by a hurricane. Things were thrown on the floor and broken everywhere. I found my laptop, but it was broken also. Blankets, pillows, kitchen utensils, and dishes had been thrown everywhere. Everything was in total disarray. I found a paper printout from my Facebook page. My picture was on it; there was a note with my first and last name, and "get him" written across the page. The police must have used this picture when they raided the house, but they could not find me. I put everything back in order in the house as best I could and called my cousin. I told him to come to the house, but he was afraid of being caught. I told him the police will never come back here because they think the same way you think and so, they won't ever come back to this place. I convinced him it would be okay, and he came.

Before long, I brought some other immigrants to the house to stay. It was a big house and it did not make sense for me to rent another house for them. I could save some money by having everyone stay in the same place. For some unknown reason, I did not care about my security anymore and did not take special caution as I resumed my smuggling activities. So, it was inevitable that one day the police would show up at my doorstep. And so, it happened that one night as my cousin and I were walking out the door that I felt something hit my head and I fell to the ground. When I opened my eyes, I saw a couple of policemen standing over me. They put a gun to my head and brought me inside the house where they handcuffed me. They ordered me to lay down on my stomach, which I did.

They started searching the house and pulled everything apart like it was when I came back there. One of the policemen started interrogating me. He asked me if I had any drugs hidden inside the house. I told him no. They asked for my ID and I gave them my fake Passport, which they immediately spotted as a phony. They were checking the IDs of the others in the house and recognized they were all fake also. I could see now that I was in very big trouble. I could not do anything about the fix I was in.

After a while, one of the policemen came and lifted me up from the floor. He took me to the other room and asked me to show him where I hid my money. I tried to convince him that I had no money stashed in the house, but if he would let me go, I

could bring him what he wanted. He told me that
he wanted $10,000 to let all of us go. I confessed that
I had some money stashed, but all I had was around
$3,000. He went out and talked with the other po-
licemen and quickly returned. He removed my
handcuffs, warning me not to do anything crazy,
and I went to my hiding place to retrieve my cash.
After he was satisfied that I had given him everything I had, he instructed us to stay put and not
leave the house for one hour. After that it would be
safe for us to leave.

After they were gone, we were all scared. I knew
we would have to move out of that house right
away, but I had been cleaned out of my money and
could not go out and rent another house that day. I
told everyone that I would have to send them out of
the country right away and they would have to give
me all their money to pay their way. They knew the
danger they were in and they quickly agreed. I got
two boats and gathered everything we would need.
It was a rush decision, but it was the only decision
that made sense at that time.

It was eight hours to the zero point, which gave
me plenty of time to think and worry along the
way. How long will this take? How long will I have

to keep running scared, watching for any trouble from the police dogging my trail. Once again, I was sensing nothing but trouble and danger all around me and closing in on me. I hated all the lies and deceit that my life had become. Everything was fake; the money I made was dirty money. I did not want it anymore. I wanted to relax and live a life without the fear and stress that come with living outside of the law.during thses years i lost my contact with giev and he longer interested talk to me, he was changed, last time i spoke with him he was telling me there is no god exist, and make me think more about that, really if god exist where is he? why he forsake us nd left us here.

When we reached the place where Halil could meet us, I called him, and he came right away to pick me up. As soon as I got in his car, he was telling me to bring him more immigrants to smuggle.

It was obvious that he had gotten hooked on the money and needed it to keep coming to keep him satisfied. I promised him I would bring more immigrants as soon as I came back. As I walked with the group to the zero point, I was thinking about what I needed to do to change the course of my life. All the way to the water I kept asking myself how long I wanted to live this way. I knew that one day I would get caught and everything would be over. I would end up in jail for who knew how long. There was no swift justice in Turkey for prisoners, especially someone who was there illegally. As we dropped the boats in the water for the refugees to leave, I made my decision: I told the family taking the first boat that I was coming with them.

CHAPTER TEN

AN UNEXPECTED GUEST IN THE CHURCH

They were happy and excited that I was coming with them and they did not have to make it on their own. The weather that night was good. The wind speed was less than eight kilometers per hour, which was the best weather you could travel by rubber boat. It only took a couple of more minutes for us to get settled into the boats and start moving forward. It was a struggle at first, but once we caught the current and were rowing together, we started going fast. I was the leader inside our boat and was steering from the bow of the boat. I looked behind us and could see the second boat was far behind us and not able to keep pace with us.

It was a different kind of fear riding on the ocean in such a small boat. On land, you can see both the countryside and the streets. At night, the headlights would show you the way and keep you on the road. But on the ocean, there were no landmarks, no roads, nothing to point the way. Still, I felt the beauty of the sea and could appreciate its power. On the ocean, I had different feelings about what might lay ahead of me. I feared what would happen if the police caught us. At the same time, I was excited about the future. I was hoping for a new destiny of freedom. I believed I was going someplace where nobody would insult me, hurt my feelings, or try to take away my freedom because of my nationality. but as i looked around i see just water, and i told my self i am like this boat, small piec in this big ocean.

We kept paddling through the night and eventually, the current took us into international waters. It was dark and scary; I realized the power of nature and how little control we had over our boats riding on the water. If the wind and tide turned against us there was no way to fight it. We were like a small piece of debris floating on this big ocean. After about three hours of riding the currents of the narrow Mytilini Strait we could see the Greek Island of Lesbos (Lesvos) ahead of us.

It was a dream for all immigrants who came this way to make it this far. The long immigrant trail that led to Istanbul was hard and full of dangers. But it was often impossible for these refugees to take the last step out of Turkey without encountering a major problem that would suddenly end their journey short of their goal. The land route from Istanbul to Greece was too well guarded by the police on both sides of the border, which made it too dangerous to get across. It was harder to get caught, and cheaper to go by sea. But it was the same story either way; anybody who took either route faced one of three possible results: cross the border safely into Greece, die trying, or be caught by the police. We were lucky. Our boat landed on the beach safely, but the other boat lagging behind us got caught by a police patrol boat before they could reach the shore. The police had a speed boat that seemed to come out of nowhere and suddenly pulled next to the other small rubber boat, almost swamping it with the big wave they made.

Although we did not share the same fate, we watched the drama unfold. We could feel how disappointed they must have been. In seconds, they totally lost all the hope that had been building in them for months as they planned and dreamed and struggled step-by-step over mountains and streams. They had crossed borders, hungry and thirsty, spending their life savings only to be stopped just short of their goal. As they were being loaded onto the police patrol boat, no one knew what would happen to them next. At that moment I felt like a parent who had been raising their children and then seeing something bad happen to them. I believe any mother would have felt the same way. I thought about all my efforts to get them out of the city and onto the boats. How I worried for their safe journey on the water. I shared their hopes and their fears crossing the water. Now it was sad to think that all the hopes they had, and all the hopes I had for them were gone. It was hard to leave them, but I knew it was time to go. We could not watch any longer because I knew the police saw us too and they might go after us next. So, we had to move away from the beach and move fast to keep from being caught too.

Once we started walking, we began to separate from each other. I was young and strong, and used to walking. So, by myself, I could walk for hours before I got tired. I knew we had a long way to go and I could not afford to hold myself back too much just so the others could keep up. We would have to walk for 24 to 36 hours, depending on how fast we could go. There were very few people on this remote part of the island and therefore no buses or taxis. All around us were nothing but woods with many wild olive trees. There were no buildings or houses anywhere in sight. We would just have to keep walking until we reached the port city of Mytilene on the southeast side of the island. We were not sure how long it would take, but we hoped we would reach the city the next night.

I had my phone with me, and fortunately, the Turkish sim cards were working here. I called Reza. He had moved to Athens to run our boss' business from the Greek mainland. I needed directions from him and he was able to tell us the right way to go. I was hoping we would not have that far to travel, but he confirmed that we would have to walk at least 36 hours. So, I prepared myself mentally to walk for at least two nights and a full day.

At first, I was able to walk at a fast pace, but once the sun rose higher, the temperature got too hot keep going at that pace. After every hour of walking, I would have to stop and rest in the shade of the trees. I had no food or water with me, so I was getting very hungry and thirsty, but I had to move on. In the daylight hours every now and then I could see a house in the distance. But I was too scared to go and ask for food or water from whomever might be there. Sometimes, I could see a car on the road going toward the city. I waved my hand to try and get them to stop and give me a ride, but no one would stop. At one point I saw truck loaded with milk that must have been taking it to the city to sell. I waved my hand again to try and make the driver stop, but he would not stop either. He just stared at me a couple of times as he passed me by.

As the day wore on, I started to get a blister on my foot, and it was making it harder and harder for me to walk. I was sure the others were tired and footsore too. It was getting dark and the temperature was dropping fast. I had been sweating all day and threw my jacket in my backpack, now the cold was getting into my bones. The night was coming fast, and I was tired from walking, but there was no place to find shelter from the cold night air middle of all olive trees. I did not know exactly where I was and could not see very far ahead of me, but I had to keep pressing forward. I kept getting calls on my phone from Turkey, but I did not have the energy to talk and walk,my cousing want to make sure i am ok, so I left the calls unanswered. I was blurry eyed and as the darkness closed in on me, I could no longer see where I was going in the dark. A few others from our group had kept up with me since we landed. We stayed together in the cold and dark until we could walk no farther and had to rest. We decided it would be best to sit close together to try and keep warm and safe until morning.

As we huddled together between a couple of trees, there seemed to be nothing but darkness all around us. We were frightened by the sound of animals howling from somewhere in the forest. Since my encounter with the bear the last time I was lost in the forest, I started carrying a knife, but it would not be much help against a big or pack of animal or protect us from the cold and dark that was enveloping us. As the night wore on, it became surprisingly cold. all of us start asking god help us if you are real, if you exsit, We had to cling to each other to try and stay warm. Later that night we saw a car approaching us. It stopped close to where we were sitting. The headlights illuminated the trees and bushes around us and suddenly made our night seem like day. A man got out of the driver's seat. We were all wondering who this person might be and what he was doing here at this time of the night. It was the middle of the night; too late to be touring around the forest. We all watched him as he stood in front of his car and started reading a pice of paper in the headlight. We all looked at each other and figured that he was not a policeman. So, we were thinking that maybe it would be alright if we asked him for help.

One of the guys in our group volunteered to go talk to him. He slowly walked up to him and started talking. The stranger was startled at first and was about to freak out, but our guy kept talking to him and calmed him down. After a minute or two, I thought maybe we too could go and talk to him. As I approached him, I could see he was wearing a long white robe and immediately realized he was a Christian priest. I reached out and shook his hand and wasted no time asking him if he could give us a ride to the city. I offered to pay him money, but he shook his head and said no, he was sorry that he could not take us. I told him in my broken English that we were tired, hungry, and thirsty and could he please help us. He turned and pointed to the darkness behind us and said we could go inside and rest. We turned our heads to where he was pointing and to our shock and amazement, we discovered that we had been sitting right in front of a church building. it was like a birthday gift for us, life saving gift, As he opened the door and invited us into the church, I could not believe that it had been there all along.

It had been more than ten years since I had been inside of a church. The last time was when my friend Give took me to church with his family back in Tehran. It was a familiar scene though, with the smell of burnt candles and the residue of incense in the air. The walls of the church were brightly decorated, and a large picture of Mary was on display. I was amazed to see this beautiful church in the middle of a wilderness. The priest told us we could stay there overnight, but it was not long after he left us there that we heard a car approaching the church. I peeked outside the window and realized that a police car had come and stopped in front of the church. Immediately, I thought that the priest had betrayed us. After locking us inside the church, he must have called the police to come right away and arrest us.

The policeman got out of his car and approached the door of the church. Just as he was about to place his hand on the door handle and step inside, something distracted him. A voice crackled over the police radio. It must have been announcing something important because he turned, jumped into his car and sped away. We watched breathlessly as the police car disappeared down the road. I was so frightened by what had happened that I wished someone could pour cold water over my head to revive me.

When the priest came back, we were ready to tell him off to his face for trying to trick us into being caught by the police. I was angry and upset and was just waiting for him to walk in the door so I could tell him just what I thought of him and treat him like others as i use to. But when he returned, his arms were full of food and bottles of water for us. My fury turned to confusion as I had to swallow my angry words in the face of his kindness to us. Now I could see clearly that he did not betray us. We thanked him for the food, but I had lost my appetite. I was angry with myself and wondered why

I judged so quickly the motivations of this priest. He only showed us kindness; he gave us a place to stay and food to eat. It must have been a coincidence that the policeman came when he did. i remember when i was 9 years old i kicked out of mosque because i was afghan eventhough i was shiia like other iraian, but why he as christian prist give me warm place food to eat and he put his self and his position to danger by hiding us.

After the priest left, I was finally calm enough to eat my food. We all needed sleep, but there was no space for us to lay down. The pews and the altar filled the church. The pews could be moved, so we put a couple next to each other and stretched out on them to sleep. I removed a cover from one of the tables to make a blanket, but it was not enough to keep me warm. I found a tray that was used to hold the candles that people burned in the church and removed all the candles from it. We brought some pieces of wood from outside and made a fire on it to warm us. It helped, but the smoke quickly filled the church, so we had to open the windows. They were trying to keep the fire going without too much smoke, as I drifted into sleep.

The next morning, I felt someone shaking me and waking me. When I pulled my sleepy head from under the cover to see who it was, I saw a woman run outside screaming. I jumped up and woke the others. Fearing she was going to call the police, I said we needed to go right away. When I looked around the church, I could see that we had totally messed everything up. The church was a wreck; our fire had completely ruined the tray we used, and everything inside the church was in disarray. We had really made a mess of things. We quickly gathered our things and tried to straighten up the clutter before we left. Just as we were about to get out of the church, the same lady returned with fresh bread in her hands for us. This was the second time I was thinking these people were going to call the police. Now I was confused. I realized that I had the habit of thinking negatively about people and assuming their reaction when seeing us was only to have us thrown in jail. I could see that it was my mindset that was all wrong and I had to get rid of it as i change my location and border. I had been judging others based on my experience and it was not good.

The bread smelled wonderful. We quickly washed our hands and faces, the water was cold fresh water from mountain and it remind me my village very morning, took some of the bread, and gobbled it up. We were very grateful to them for their kindness. I will never forget the taste of the bread that lady brought to us. It was the taste of hope and love given to strangers, and not any normal bread. After we ate, we said goodbye to them and left the church. As the church disappeared behind us, I started thinking, "Okay. Tonight, we need to reach the city." It was not long before we were feeling weary and exhausted once again. I felt we could not stay outside another night. We all needed a good meal and some sleep.

Right after leaving the church, I called Reza again and told him were we were. He told me we were another eight hours away from the closest bus station. He knew this place so well that it seemed like he must have traveled this way ten times. my phon charger keep giving my messge it is going out of energy as we do, But in truth, he had never been here before. All he did was check the Google map every time we called. Every day he was doing the same for different groups like ours and had become

114

an expert about this route. Sure enough, we arrived at the bus station late afternoon, after eight hours of walking. A bus to the city left that station every three hours. While I waited, other refugees started straggling into the station. When our bus arrived, we all moved to the back of the bus and sat together on the last and biggest seat available. All the way to the city people kept staring at us, but we did not care. We did not believe that anyone was going to call the police to come and catch us. When we finally reached the outskirts of the city, I thanked God for bringing us to the end of this very difficult journey. From the bus station, we took a car into the city.

I could see the beautiful ocean in the distance. I could see big ships and many small sailing boats all around the harbor. It seemed like paradise all around me. Mytilene would have been a nice place to visit. It is one of the oldest port cities in the world and has a long pier to protect its harbor. A medieval castle can be seen from the harbor and the city view is dominated by the dome of a church. Unfortunately, we could not stay there. It is a small city with only a couple of wide streets. I was surprised to see so many women driving bikes – a sight not seen in places where I had been before.

We knew this place has one of the biggest refugee camps in Greece. Most refugees that survive the ocean trek will end up being caught on Lesbos. If it takes them more than a few days to get on board of one of the boats to the mainland of Greece, they will be detained in the refugee camp and fingerprinted. After that their journey will be over because which country they go, the police will soon find out that they have fingerprints in Greece, and they will send them back to the camp here.

At first, we were just walking around the city without knowing where we should go to get our boat tickets. I found a barber and wanted to get a haircut and take a shower but could only get a haircut. After the barber was finished, I did not feel any cleaner because he did not wash my hair.the only place i missed middle east cultur,barbers wash your haird after haircut. When we tried to get our boat tickets to Athens, they refused to sell them to us, and turned us away because none of us had a visa or passport to show. To turn away suspicion from us, I told them that my papers were in my hotel, but looking into their eyes, I could tell that they did not

116

believe my phony story. When one of them started to pick up a phone and call someone, we ran out, afraid we were about to be arrested. It was almost 7 PM and we were still walking around the town without any way of leaving the island.

When I called Reza, he had no good news for us either. His only advice for us was to go to the police station and give ourselves up. He said they would send us to the refugee camp where we would be fingerprinted and kept for two weeks. Upon being released, we would be given papers identifying us as refugees. Those papers would allow us to travel to Athens without any trouble. I told him he was crazy if he thought after all I had been through – crossing the sea on a rubber boat, hiding out inside a church, and walking for days across that island – that I would just give myself up. "I'll never do that," I said and hung up on him. I was starting to think that it would be impossible to get off that island. But, if I stayed there much longer, I would be finished. If they won't sell me a ticket, they won't allow me to use the banking system either. Once I spent all my money, there was no bank that would allow an illegal person to transfer some money. Still, I promised myself that I was not going to surrender and end up in a refugee camp. I would have to find some way to get off the island, but how? but i really scared,it was a Beautifull island, the place i just was on magazin and tv, but slowly become jail for me, i cann't blieve i stuck here inside this place and i had no where to go. but i knw the place i can ask for help and it worked last time, i ask god help me please, i will be a ood person i promiss no crime anymore.

CHAPTER ELEVEN

FREEDOM TICKET

As the day came to an end, we had spent the day with no success. We found an Internet club where we could spend part of the night just cruising the Internet to pass the time and stay out of the cold night air. The place closed at one o'clock in the morning and we had to leave. Before leaving I had to pay the highest cost for Internet access in my entire life: I could not believe I was paying almost 30 Euros for only a couple of hours sitting in front of a computer. this is another thing i really think about my country, 30 Euros was my dad sallery for a month.

We found a park not far from the club and looked around to find a place where we could sit or sleep for the night. My traveling companions had lost hope and said they were going to find a police station where they could turn themselves in to the immigration authorities. I tried to talk them out of it, but they could not stand another night in the cold with nowhere to go and no way to reach the mainland of Greece and no church and prist to save us. I told them that I was not going with them. I was going to stay right there whatever happened. After they left, I kept looking around for somewhere to sleep. As they say, "seek and you shall find ask you shall recieve" and I found a large empty refrigerator carton and a TV carton that had been left beside a trashcan. I emptied all the trash from the large carton and went into box to sleep. I made a makeshift tee shirt or sleeping bag from a large trash bag by making a small hole in the bottom big enough for my head to squeeze through. Then, at last, I settled down to sleep. It turned out to be the nicest sleep I could remember for a long time. I did not know how long I slept or why I was able to sleep so well, but my slumber was abruptly ended by the sound of a dog barking just above my head. His owner was curious about what was inside the box, but quickly turned and ran away when we he saw me come out of the box.

I was not concerned by the stranger and his dog finding me. I found a place to wash my face and left to go eat some breakfast. Just then, I saw my other traveling companions sleeping in the park. They had taken what shelter they could in front of the door, hoping that maybe someone would come along and open the door for them, but they were not so lucky this time. I asked them why they decided to come back. They found out that during the winter months the camp does not accept anyone from inside the island. Once anyone made it this far, they had to figure out on their own how to get off the island. The camp is only for people who were captured at sea and never made it to shore in the first place.

We decided to go to the place near the shore where they sold tickets for the ships leaving port. But again, we had no success trying to buy our tickets without a single passport among us. We started walking along the beachfront, not knowing what to do next when I felt something biting and pulling on my leg. I turned and saw a small black dog attacking my leg. He was snarling at me, looking into my eyes, and pulling on my leg with all his might. I started screaming for help, but nobody came near me. Not a moment too soon, the dog released my leg from his jaws, bolted away from me, and ran down the beach. I could see that my pants leg was torn all the way down to my shoe, and my leg was bleeding. I did not know where I could get any medical attention. So, I just found a place to rest for a while until I stopped bleeding.

I was more concerned with finding a way to get out of that place than I was with finding treatment for my wounded and bloodied leg. While walking around, I ran into another one of the guys from our group. He told me that on the night before, after they had been turned away from the refugee camp, they stopped at a gas station to get something to eat. The woman working there gave them some free food. She seemed like a very nice woman and my friend thought maybe she could help us. I thought we had nothing to lose and asked him to show me the gas station.

We had to walk almost an hour to reach it, and when we arrived, that same woman looked at us and started to give us chips and cookies. I told her that we did not need snacks but were in desperate need of her help in another way. She was a very nice lady and asked me what was it that we needed.

I explained to her that we were stuck there, and we needed help to go to Athens. We needed someone to buy tickets for us because no one will sell them to us because we have no passports or identity cards. She thought for a moment, reached for her phone, and called someone who must have been related to her. She passed the phone to me and the man just told me to go the refugee camp. I didn't argue with him and just hung up the phone. I was very emotional at that moment and told the lady to look at my leg. I lied and told her the police did it to me. I scolded her, "You guys have no mercy." Just then she started crying and called the same man again and asked him to please come and help us. After a few minutes, a handsome man pulled into the gas station driving a nice sports car. She told me to go with him and he will buy a ticket for me. At that moment, I felt like the happiest person in the world. I thanked her and kissed her hand. From the way she responded, I don't think she had ever seen anyone so grateful or had her hand kissed like that.

My friend and I jumped into the car and he drove us to the city. On the way he asked me how many tickets I needed. When I told him seven, he stopped the car suddenly and asked, "seven?" I told him yes, I have six friends and they are all waiting for me in the city. He was stunned when we arrived at the city park and I showed him all my friends waiting there. He shook his hand at me and told me how much it would cost him. He did not think we had any money. But when I pulled a thousand Euros from my pocket, he calmed down. He looked at the money, then looked at me, surprised, and said, "Oh, you have money." I had to explain again, that I had plenty of money for our tickets, but no ID. I gave him the money for the tickets, and he asked me to wait in the car. "Don't come out or roll down the windows. I don't want anyone to see you guys."

He came back a few minutes later with seven tickets in his hand. We just smiled and thanked him with all our hearts. He dropped us off at the park and drove away. When I gathered everyone together and told them I had tickets for all of them, they jumped for joy and started screaming and kissing me. I told them there was no time for celebrations; our tickets were for six o'clock that evening and the time was already one o'clock in the afternoon. We had to split up so we would not draw attention to ourselves when we boarded the ship.

After one hour we reached the area where the ships loaded their passengers. I thought, before trying to board our ship I had better have something to eat. I found a restaurant close to the docks and as I ate, I watched the passengers boarding the two o'clock ship. I suddenly realized that there were policemen standing at the door to the ship and they were checking everyone for passports and identification papers. I thought, "Oh my god, how can we get onto the ship now?" At every step we faced a new challenge. We had our tickets, but now how will we get past the police?

I finished eating my lunch and figured I had another four hours to find a way onto our ship or I would never make it off that island. I was walking around the port and watching the activities on the docks. Around two o'clock I saw one big ship come into port and dock nearby. After they had opened the doors, I realized this ship was the one we were supposed to be going on. I saw one open door on the ship that no one was watching. When the moment seemed right, I quickly jumped through the door and was inside the ship.

I started up the stairs to the passenger area and saw one of the ship's officers coming down the stairs in front of me. He looked at me and asked me what I was doing there. I showed him my ticket and told him I was looking for a bathroom. He took my ticket, cut it and told me the bathrooms were up-stairs. After he left, I ran into the bathroom and closed the door. I just sat there for a moment, re-lieved that I had made it onboard. I immediately got on the phone and called my friends to warn them that they needed to come to the ship right away and find a way to get onboard before the po-lice started checking people at the door. "You need to come early," I told them, "otherwise you will not be able to get onto the ship. The police control the main door and will not let anyone onboard without proper identification."

Rather than thanking me for the warning, they were mad, "You left us alone?" I said, "I got you guys your tickets. You cannot expect me to do eve-rything else for you." I hung up my phone and turned it off. It was not long before I heard the en-gines on the ship starting up. Once the ship started moving away from the dock, I looked outside to see if any of my friends made it onboard. I saw one of my friends on the dock in handcuffs. Only one of my friends was able to make it past the security and was safely onboard. The others had been caught by the police. There was nothing I could do about that now I thought. I needed to stop worrying about those I left behind and start looking ahead. I turned and went inside the ship to find a place to wait until we reached Athens.

CHAPTER TWELVE

REAL FACE OF EUROP

I was amazed by what I saw when I walked around to the bow of the ship. I was on a cruise ship with all the luxuries provided to make the tourists happy. Onboard there was a swimming pool and a playground for children, a media center with televisions, a bar, a dance club, and more. I decided to sit and watch TV just to pass the time, but I was not really enjoying myself. I was on this ship for a different reason than the rest of the tourists around me. I had to be on my guard because I did not want to be caught traveling as an illegal immigrant.

I met other immigrants on the ship that had been released from the refugee camp on Lesbos.

They had been given their papers permitting them to go to the mainland. They were astonished that I made it onto the ship without any of the necessary papers. I asked them to share their stories with me and learned that all of them had gone through different trials to get so far, and i hope one day they can write their own storys so prople can read them. The one thing we all had in common was we all had to learn how to be suspicious and not trust anyone. When anyone enters another country illegally, they must learn to mistrust everyone and everything. No one is a friend of an illegal and once they know about you, they will try to take advantage of your situation. They told me to be careful when it was time to exit the boat because they would ask me for my documents before I got off. But I was lucky. And I was able to get off the boat the same way I got on with no problem. i learned alot techniques while i was smugling and i was smart enoughe to handle any situation.

As soon as I was off the boat, I called Reza, but he was not in Athens. However, he gave me the number of some Afghan people he knew that were renting a house in the city and had been there for a long time. I called the number and talked to the guy about my situation. From the tone of his voice and what he was telling me, he seemed like a good person. So, I took a taxi to his house. When I approached the area where he lived, I could not believe my eyes. Every house in that neighborhood was a refugee house. This area of Athens is called Exarchia. It sits between the University of Athens and the Politechnion and is home to students, immigrants, and Greek families of different economic strata. It is famous for its immigrant restaurants, cafes, and computer shops. Arabic or Farsi signs are everywhere in the shop windows and businesses. I could see on the balconies of apartments all around me washed clothes hung out to dry.

When I found the house I was looking for, it had multiple rooms with a big courtyard. It was perfectly suited to be a place for refugees to stay. It was lovely for me to experience the smells of home cooking coming from the kitchen. When I entered the kitchen, I saw a couple of people cooking food in a large pot. I did not know how many people were staying in the house, but they must have been making a meal for a large group. An old man came to greet me and as soon as I sat down with him, he told me the costs for me to stay there.

I accepted the prices without haggling with him. He showed me to my room, and I asked where the bathroom was so I could take a much needed shower. I had to borrow shampoo and soap but was happy to be clean and fresh again and smells good again. I went to my room and immediately fell into a deep sleep. It was dark when I woke up. I could hear the cheers of a big crowd outside of my room watching a football match on the Television. I washed my face and went downstairs to join them. I saw a couple of the refugees sitting with the group that I sent from Turkey a couple of months before. When they saw me, they stood up and hugged me. Then they brought me some tea, and we sat down to talk. A few minutes later they brought some nice food for us to share.

It had been some time since I had the pleasure of sitting with a big group of friends and eating together. Since leaving home, I was almost always alone. I had gotten used to going to good restaurants and eating expensive food, but I always had to watch my back. Whenever I was outside of my house in Istanbul, I had to worry about my security. I had to be wary of the police coming and questioning me; the stress of my lifestyle always spoiled the taste of my food. But as I sat there eating my food surrounded by this company, I could savor every bite because I was not having to worry about anything. It was like my first taste of freedom in a long, long time.

After a couple of days rest, I was talking with Reza about my plan to escape to Italy. I did not want to waste too much time in Athens but planned to move on as soon as possible. Reza was staying in another Greek city called Patras. Patras overlooks a Gulf on the northern Peloponnese, 215 km west of Athens. Patras is a major seaport, so there are a lot of ships coming and going from all around the world. Since the harbor can accommodate the big ships that carry cargo to ports all over Europe, it makes it a popular destination for refugees. They pay smugglers to help them hide inside of trucks and cargo containers on ships going to England, France, Italy, and other European ports. Some refugees have been known to end up back in Pakistan if they did not understand where they were going.

I had to go by train to meet Reza. Because it is necessary to show ID to ride the trains in Europe, I had to plan carefully how to get onto the train without being caught without proper identification.

It took careful timing and a little bit of luck, but I was able get on the train without any trouble. I called Reza to come and pick me up when the train arrived at the station near him. Before boarding the train, I decided to dress up in nice clothes, so I shaved and wore a new suit jacket that i purchased. When I got off the train, Reza wearing a black hat with black clothes and was carrying a black backpack, he looks like a thief, but actually we have to admit, we are thief sneaking to this country without permisison,i remember the famouse quote from afghan authore kite runner book it says There is only one sin, only one. And that is theft. (Here comes the explanation) Every other sin is a variation of theft... When you kill a man, you steal a life.You steal his wife's right to a husband, rob his children of a father. When you tell a lie, you steal someone's right to the truth. When you cheat, you steal the right to fairness. There is no act more wretched than stealing.

I hugged him as soon as we met and started talking to him, but suddenly he started running, turned to me and told me to run. At first, I did not understand what was going on, but as soon as I saw a police car stop right beside me and the policemen inside looking at me, I realized that the police were watching the train station for any illegals traveling through their city to find a way onto one of the many ships that were leaving the port every day. I started running right behind Reza, but I had no idea where we were running to. We were just running to get away from the police that were chasing us. It was not easy for me because I had no experience of playing "cat and mouse" with the police nipping at my heels.

I was able to keep pace with Reza and followed his every move. He was helping me, showing me where I needed to go as we jumped from house to house and sprinted from street to street. But the police were following us wherever we went. No doubt, Reza had become expert at this kind of marathon, but the police were pros too. We finally lost them by laying down between the rails of a train line and hugging the metal so they could not see us. After lying still for a few minutes, everything was quiet again. Reza stood up and told me to follow him.

I asked him what was going on in this place. He described the whole situation like being in an action movie. Refugees had to be on guard every day because the police were looking for anyone that looked suspicious. But this time the police went right after us, because of me. I asked, "Why because of me?" He told me that only smugglers dress up like you and immigrants have old clothes like me. As we walked and talked along the train line, I began to realize why he dressed the way he did. He was telling me how different his situation was now. He was tired of running but did not know what to do. He was not working with his old boss in Turkey any longer and had become independent. I could see that he was hopeless, miserable, and had lost his way.

After walking a short distance, we reached a wooded area, and as we walked farther into the trees, I could see lights in the distance. We reached a clearing and I found myself inside a small camp of immigrants living in the woods. I remembered one night in Turkey when I was showed a similar camp of immigrants. Reza told me that almost three hundred Afghan refugees were living in this camp and some had been there almost five years. They don't have any place to go and are just stuck here. They have no money and no jobs. They must steal food from the markets or rummage through the trash cans just to be able to survive. That is why the police do not like to see us walking around inside the city. He explained that all these refugees lived inside the tent city and every tent was designed to hold up to four persons, but some of them have as many as ten people living inside of them. They were truly a small village with a billiard hall, Internet café, and video game arcade. And of course, they had to pay the smugglers to use any of them. But they did not have any running water. So, they had to use the woods for toilet and bathing, which explained why it smelled so bad around the camp.

When we reached Reza's tent and went inside, I discovered it was just a bare floor and we were sitting on the ground. I asked Reza where he slept and he replied, "Right here. In the summer it gets hot and the winter it's too cold, but we had use it. The most comfortable tents belong to the smugglers. They were living in an RV that they bought in the city and parked in the campsite. Inside the RV they have a TV, kitchen, and bathroom; it was like a small apartment in there. I noticed that many of the tents had a small satellite dish and thought it odd that they did not have a bathroom or restroom, but they did have satellite TV.

I was very tired from the train ride, the chase through the city, and the long walk to the camp so I decided to lay down on the ground inside the tent and sleep. The ground was hard, and my body was itching all over, but after a couple of hours of tossing and turning, I finally settled down and slept. I was awakened suddenly by a big commotion outside our tent. I jumped up and looked outside to see what was going on. A large crowd of Afghans were fighting each other. It was like a movie, but real. I asked one of the other onlookers what was going on and he told me it was a fight between Hazaras and Pashtuns. This was part of an ethnic conflict going back centuries. The Hazara people are Shiie Muslims, and the Pashtun people are Sunni Muslims. Even in refugee camps like this one, the ancient conflict is still going on.

What happened this time and who started the fight and why I did not know, but it quickly got out of hand and now the special riot police were surrounding the camp. They brought special bulldozers with them and were threatening to destroy the whole camp if the people did not stop fighting. After the policeman in charge made an announcement that everybody should go back inside their tents, the fight was quickly over. The other resident of the camp that I was talking with told me that every morning some anti-government group brings food and drink to the people in the camp and try to stir up the crowd to join in protests. It would not be long before the factions inside the camp start fighting each other. It seemed strange to me that these refugees would fight over a few scraps of food when so many of them carried hundreds (or in some cases thousands) of dollars with them for their travel expenses. Most refugees carefully planned their journey and would sell family property or carry their life savings with them before they left home. A couple of people had been badly injured in the fight, and police took them to a hospital. After everyone calmed down and order was restored, the police pulled back.

I am sure they are trying to come up with a solution to the refugee crisis in Greece and rid themselves of these camps once and for all.

It hurt me to see the conditions in this camp. There was much I wanted to say about it, but I thought it best not to. I was already planning my next move. I passed the day talking with Reza about the best way to get to Italy from there. I told him that I did not want to stay there very long. I was afraid of contracting a disease or sickness from all the unsanitary conditions in the camp. Reza said the only way to Italy was to be smuggled on board a cargo ship. He would help me find the best truck to hide in that was being loaded onto a ship to Italy.

I knew this part of my trip would be very difficult to plan and timing would have to be just right. We would have to deal with many different problems and dangers to be smuggled out of Greece and into Italy. Anything was possible; I could be hit and killed by one of the trucks being loaded onboard, or I could suffocate to death in the back of sealed truck or cargo container. Sometimes they hid refugees in the back of refrigerated trucks carrying food and they would die from being exposed for too long to freezing temperatures. But I was ready to face all those dangers if it meant I was able to be far away from here and make it to Europe.

It was late at night when Reza told me and a couple of others to change clothes and get ready to go. I dressed the way Reza told me and looked like him or like any other homeless refugee. We walked all the way to the port to the staging area where all the trucks were parked while waiting their turns to be loaded onto cargo ships. This area had some of the strictest security I had ever seen. Tall walls surrounded the entrance and every possible way in. On to top of the walls, security cameras were everywhere, watching anyone who approached the walls. There was only one way to go; so, we had to pass through all this security without being seen. I had no idea how other immigrants did it, but we found a way to quickly climb the walls and slip past the cameras without being caught. We had some friends help us by acting like immigrants trying to sneak in to decoy the security away from their posts. So, they were too busy chasing them to see us. Once we got inside, Reza showed his expertise as a smuggler and quickly identified which trucks were going to Europe and which were not. He read the tags and tag stickers until he found the ideal truck for me to get inside. We swiftly hugged each other farewell and I promised to send him some money as soon as I made it to the other side. Reza broke the seal and I got inside. I suddenly realized that this truck was full of immigrants just like me. I told Reza that there were already two families inside that truck, and it was too risky for me to join them. So, we passed on that one. He carefully replaced the seal and we went looking for another one.

The next truck we found going my way, I could only find a place to hide underneath the truck. It was a very tight squeeze, but it seemed safe. I did not know how many hours I would have to hide myself in that position before I reached the end of this voyage. Not long after Reza left, the truck driver came and started the engine. He drove the truck onto the cargo ship and soon I would be on my way to Italy. It was totally dark in the cargo hold of the ship, but after a while I could hear the muffled voices of some other refugees that had been smuggled onto this same truck. I realized they must be hidden somewhere inside the truck, but I could not tell exactly where they might be.

After a few hours the ship's engine shut down and everything got very quiet. Then the cargo doors were opened. What happened next was big surprise. I could hear the barking of police dogs. They were sniffing everywhere, and soon they were right next to me. They were looking for and finding immigrants being smuggled on the trucks. As soon as the dog reached my hiding place, I saw its big face right in front of me and its sharp teeth snapping at me. Its handler held back the dog to keep it from biting me, while the police removed me from the truck along with a couple others that were hidden inside the driver's cabin. I don't know how they got in there, but their smuggler must have been a pro.

The police took all of those they could find outside the ship and held us in custody. It was the first time I could smell the fresh air of freedom in Italy. It reminded me of the first time I stepped out into the fresh air of Istanbul. I was enjoying the nice weather and looking all around me to see as much of Italy that I could from the harbor. I could imagine myself in just a few hours, walking down some street in Rome. One of the other Afghans next to me said he wasn't scared because now that we are here there was no way they could send us back. They will just take our fingerprints, release us, and let us stay here. I told him I did not plan to stay here but wanted to go all the way to England.

Eventually, the police officer in charge came into the room and ordered the other officer to take us back to the same ship we arrived on, lock us in a room, and send us back to Greece. I was shocked and started to argue with the officer. "You can't send us back!" I insisted, "It would be illegal." He

142

looked at me with distain, and said, "Illegal?" You are illegal." I did not have a word to answer him. They put us all in the same room on the ship. All our hopes were dashed to pieces. Who would want to come back this way again? I was so completely fed up with everything that I had experienced since arriving in Greece that I told myself as soon as I got the chance, I was going back to Turkey. I was thinking, "I will never come back here again."

CHAPTER THIRTEEN

GOD CHANGED MY PLANS

A s we sat in that small room on the ship back to Patras, some people were crying, and some were angry. Although I was determined never to go back to Europe, others were longing to come back and try again as soon as they could. Listening to everyone around me, I was not persuaded to try again; something in my heart was telling me, "Don't come back. Go back to Turkey." When I told the others, I was set on going back to Turkey, they were stunned and thought I was crazy to go back after having struggled so hard to come this far. But I told them my mind was made up; I was going. I could not explain it, but I felt something inside of me telling me I had to go back. This was not the way I needed to go.

When our ship got back to same port in Greece, there was no red carpet waiting for us. They unceremoniously kicked us off the ship. The second the police saw us, they started chasing us through the streets towards the refugee camp. Once again, I had escaped the arms of the police and ended back at Reza's tent. I was tired and depressed, but I knew I could not stay in this camp one more day.

I searched the camp for Reza, but he was not there. I changed my clothes and went outside to walk around and see if I could find someone to talk to about how to get back to Istanbul.

I saw a person I knew from Turkey. He was a young guy and knew me well. But as soon as he saw me walking toward him, he turned and went the other way. I called his name and chased him, but he just ran away. I knew why he did not want to talk to me. His name was navid. I remember the first time I saw him was when ahmad brought him to our house from the immigrant safe house. I asked him why he did that. He knew it was dangerous to bring the immigrants we were smuggling to our house, but he would not listen. I knew that ahmad was sick and he like to have sex with younger boys it is called bachabaz(playboy), but it seemed that

145

this young man did not know why he was being brought to our house. I don't know what happened that night, but that guy never talked to me afterwards. Although I guessed the reason why he was running from me now, it still hurt me personally. I wanted to help him somehow. I wished I could have told him something to release him from his shame. I wished I could have gone back to that first night I saw him and helped him then, but I did not do anything when I had the chance.

The journey that immigrants travel is a life changing experience. Sometimes the experiences hurt and damage them for life and sometimes all the pain and sufferings are rewarded at the end of their journey. Anyone who sets off on this journey needs to be prepared for both; either way, it will change their life forever. Only one thing seemed certain to me: this way of life is unforgiving, and people will have no mercy on you – especially if you are weak.

This encounter with navid was just another sign to me that I could not stay in Greece any longer. I had to go back that very night. So, I went to the train station, bought my ticket, and traveled back to Athens. I called Reza several times, but he did not answer his phone. I was worried about him, but it was time for me to board the train. Back in Athens, I found the same house I stayed in before and called my old boss back in Turkey. I asked him if he knew someone who could help me, and he did. One of his captains and another smuggler working for him were in Greece, but they were going back to Istanbul soon. He would call them and tell them to bring me back with them. I gave him my number and told him I would be waiting for their call.

The one who called me the next morning was from Afghanistan too. His name was Hakan and he told me where I needed to meet him. I said my goodbyes to everyone in the house I was staying, but they could not believe I was really going back. They thought I was making a big mistake, but I was 100% sure that I had to go. There was nothing more for me in Greece; it was a dead end for me. I found Hakan and the captain my boss said would help me. The captain looked like a Rambo character. He had a muscular build with many scars on his face and body that made him look like he had survived many battles. We wasted no time and hopped on the train that would take us to the boarder.

It was only a couple hours before we reached the closest city to the Turkish border. Every time I approached the border of one of the countries I was about to enter illegally, I would get nervous and feel afraid, but by this time, I was getting used to it. Hakan turned to me and told me to be careful because this place is totally different from being in a big city. Every person we would encounter between there and the border lived there. We had to be especially careful of the police around there because the government gives them a special reward if they catch smugglers.

I told him that I understood and would be careful. We went to a restaurant to have some food and wait until dark. From there we walked to the bus station and found the bus that would take us to the last station near the border with Turkey. It took almost two hours to reach the last station and by that time no one else was left inside the bus. It was totally dark when we stepped outside the bus and started walking toward the border. I had no idea where we were going. I just put my trust in them and kept walking. Eventually, we came to a deserted flatland that stretched into the darkness ahead of us. Hakan told me that there was a river just ahead of us, and we had to run and keep on running until we reached it. "Don't think about stopping or resting, and don't quit." I told him I wouldn't stop, "I'm not a quitter."

Hakan explained that we were not running from the police, but we had to run because there was an army of mosquitos between here and the river. The mosquitos there were huge and if you stop running, they will kill you in a couple of minutes. They will keep biting and sucking your blood until you are too weak walk or even stand up. "So, just beware," he said. I asked him why he did not tell me before then. I could have brought extra clothing for protection and some crème to block mosquitos. He told me he tried to buy some insect repellent at the last moment but could not find any. So, we would just have to run as fast as possible. He gave a short countdown. As soon as he reached the end, he pressed me forward, and I started running as fast as I could. After only a few seconds, I felt something going into my eyes and my exposed skin was being bitten. Coming out of the darkness, I could see swarms of mosquitos flying all around us and swooping down on us. I thought, "Oh my God, what is this?" I had never seen that many mosquitos concentrated in one place. They were going wild, attacking us. There was nothing we could do to defend ourselves or get rid of them. I just kept going as fast as possible and tried to ignore them as they kept stinging and biting me.

Finally, I could see some trees on the other side of the mosquito-infested marsh we were running through. I was not feeling well, and my vision was getting blurry. I could tell that I had been weakened by all the bites, but I still had to find the strength to run some more. Once we entered the trees, I found it hard to stand on my feet. My companions had to hold me up so I could walk a little farther and reach a safe place. They gave me some water to drink and we rested for a few minutes, but they told me that we had to keep moving. We could not waste any more time staying there. I was barely able to walk, but we still had a river to cross. My traveling companions had brought a small rubber boat with them and they were filling it with air so the moment we reached the bank of the river we would be ready to cross.

The captain managed to secure a rope on the opposite bank of the river and instructed us to keep our feet inside the rubber boat, hold onto the rope,

MEHDI

and pull ourselves to the other side of the river. It was a struggle to keep our balance, but it was the best way to cross.

Once we were across the river, they told me we are in Turkey now. I finally was able to breathe a sigh of relief, knowing I had made my way out of Greece.

We were about to move away from the river when I heard the voice of a woman and a crying baby nearby. We had no idea who it could be. I thought for a moment that I was confused, and it was something else, or maybe an animal crying. But the more we listened, we realized it was indeed a baby crying. We moved in the direction of the voice and discovered a family hiding in the bushes. They were just sitting there – lost and scared. We tried to talk to them, but they were too frightened of us and refused to talk to us. We figured they must have thought we were police or that we wanted to harm them. We kept talking to them and assuring them that we did not want to do them any harm. Finally, the woman started talking to us in an Arabic dialect and we could tell they were from Iraq.

They were trying to go to the Greek side of the river, but their boat had a hole in it and would not hold any air. So, the husband, wife, and three kids were just stuck there. It was a heartbreaking image to see them there – helpless, lost, and unable to go forward, but afraid of being caught if they tried to go back. So, they just sat there in the mud, kids crying, and in total despair. I told our captain that I was going to help them. Hakan and the captain quickly agreed that we ought to help them cross the river in our boat.

We guided them to our boat and gave them instructions about how to handle the rope and pull themselves across the water. The husband was strong and would be able to make it okay, but the women and her kids would be trouble. The captain put the three kids into our boat, jumped into the water, and holding onto the boat, he pushed them to the other side of the river. Although the river was not deep, the water was fast and would knock anyone off their feet if they did not have something to hold onto. And once off your feet, the current would carry you away. I will never forget the captain's brave action and sacrifice to help strangers on their way.

The captain came back to help the woman next so she could stay with the children. We helped her into the boat, and she was holding onto the rope as instructed, but she was scared and panicked as soon as the boat left the riverbank. She had only gone a few feet before she let go of the rope and immediately fell into the river. All I could see were her hands. She was drowning as the current carried her down river. Her children were screaming and crying and running down the riverbank behind her in hopes of catching her. We were also running behind her, trying to catch her.

She was lucky. She got hung up on a tree branch stuck in the middle of the river. The captain jumped into the river to rescue her, but he had to ignore her husband screaming at him, telling him not to touch his wife. I turned and looked the husband in the face and said, "She is dying! What the heck are you saying?" I got angry, shook my fist at him and told him to shut up or I would punch him. He got quiet and the captain took hold of his wife and pushed her to the other side of the river. Once his wife was safe, the man used the rope to pull himself to the other side of the river, but it was obvious that he was not happy. Rather than being relieved that his wife and children were safe, he was just yelling at his wife and kids. But we were happy because we knew we did what we were supposed to do in that situation. As we turned to go on our way, I was wondering why these people would want to live in Europe with this backward mentality.

We walked slowly toward a big farm and the village just beyond. Once we made it to the village, Hakan called his friend and asked him to pick us up. His friend had a house in the village, and it was not long before we were sitting in front of a wood stove and listening to the crackle of burning wood. The only thing I really needed was a place to get warm, but he gave us some delicious Turkish food to eat as well. We spent the night there; our captain was soaking wet from the river rescue and needed to dry out. We woke early the next morning and were fed a nice breakfast before we were given a ride to the bus station where we would find our way to Istanbul. A couple of hours later and I was back in Istanbul where I started from weeks before.

I called my boss to let him know I was back and see if he had any instructions for me. He told me a group of about 90 refugees had just arrived and he wanted me to manage them. He had acquired a flat on the fifth floor of an apartment building and wanted me to go and take care of them. I really had no choice but to agree to do what he asked. So, I got the address and went to meet them.

I found the apartment and called the number my boss gave me. The guy who answered, opened the door for me and I went inside. As it turned out, everyone in the apartment was from Pakistan and since I did not speak the language, it was a challenge for me to communicate with any of them. This was really a place for Yunus to manage, but, for as long as he was locked up in jail, I would have to take responsibility for them. I sat down in the main room of the apartment, and looked around, contemplating how I was to overcome this challenge of poor communication with the group while learning how to manage them when I heard a big bang at the front door to the apartment. A squad of special police broke through the door and came rushing inside. They were placing everyone under arrest and asked them who the smuggler was. They quickly pointed me out.

A police officer saw me and said, "Hello, Mr. Mehdi." I don't know how they knew my name, but it was certain that I was now on their watchlist and my career in Istanbul as a smuggler was over. Some of the police were talking among themselves while others were searching other rooms. I thought, "I am not going to jail." I had family and I did not come back to Turkey from Greece just to end up in jail. I was thinking, "God, did you really want this? Is this why you told me to come back?"

I was more afraid than I had ever been before in my life. I could see myself locked inside a dirty, stinking, jail cell for God knows how long. At that moment, I realized I was sitting at a window that led to the balcony of the apartment. When the police were not looking, I tied my shoes, opened the window, and climbed out onto the balcony. I used a chair and climbed up to the roof and started running. I could hear the police right behind me saying, "He is on the roof. Get him!" I was running and jumping from rooftop to rooftop with the police not far behind me. At last I came to a dead end. There was no escape and the next building was too far away for me to jump.

I was desperately looking for an escape, but time was short. The police were coming fast. There was a small ledge of about five inches just below me and I went down from the roof and hung on.

When I looked down, I saw a tree way down on the street below. I told myself, I was not going to jail and jumped in a frantic attempt to land in the tree and break my fall before I was killed landing on the pavement on the street below. After a couple of seconds, I heard a frightening loud noise from my right leg as it hit something on the way down and I landed on the street. When I woke up, I saw police standing over me, an ambulance, and people from every window above staring at me. I was in a daze. What happened to me? What had I done?

CHAPTER FOURTEEN

RUNNING FOR MY LIFE

I passed out again and woke up again inside the ambulance. I looked around and saw them working away on me. I remembered being upset because they were cutting my new pants and shirt I had just bought, and they were gone in a moment. The next time I woke up I was inside a room full of light and the Dr. was cutting my hair. Then they shaved my head, put something in front of my mouth and I went to sleep.

I don't know how long I was out, but when I woke up, I did not remember anything exactly. I saw a nurse in front of me running and calling for a doctor as she checked my eyes. I could not remember what had happened to me. When the doctor came in, he asked me if I could remember my name and where I was from. I said I knew who I was and where I was from, but I did not know where I was and could not remember why I was there. The doctor told me I had jumped from the fifth floor window of a building and broke my right hand and shoulder; I hit my head and they had to do brain surgery; my right foot and left shin were shattered. He told me it was amazing that I was alive after that such a big hit.

I looked at myself laying in the bed and saw I was bandaged completely. I could barely move. Even if I had wanted to kill myself at that moment, I would have needed help. After a couple of hours of being conscious again, I started to remember some of the details of what had happened to me. When I jumped from the window ledge, I hit my foot against the wall. There was a tree below, but what I could not see was a wall under the branches. So, when I crashed through the branches, I hit the wall and… well, there I was in the hospital bandaged from head to toe. My entire body hurt, and I had multiple broken bones.

Because I was confined to the hospital, they did not send me to the jail. The doctors and nurses treating me had no idea when I would be able to leave the hospital, but after a few days, the policeman sent to guard me put a handcuff on me and told me I could not walk around without his permission. One policeman stood in front of my room and checked on me on a regular basis. All day long I was crying over my situation and could not understand how I ended up in such a terrible condition. When I finally got a chance to call my mom, she was crying over me as always, but I did my best to assure her that I would recover and would be alright. I felt tired and was on pain medication which made me sleep a lot. But, in my waking hours, I could not help but see how everything went wrong from the time I went to Greece. I felt it was wrong to go, and now I felt it was wrong for me to come back. I was thinking that I had been lied to and deceived to come back to Istanbul and now this happened to me.

A few more days passed, and the police removed the handcuffs from me. And at the same time, they disappeared without saying a word to me. Suddenly, I was not being guarded by anyone. I could not walk anyway, and both of my legs hurt badly. It would take a long time before my legs would heal and I would be able to walk again. I had days to think about my past and future. Laying there in my hospital bed, I was feeling lost; I had forgotten what my purpose was in leaving home. I had made a lot of money and bought a lot of things for myself and my family, but I did not have any peace. I had done a lot of things wrong. I earned money the wrong way. I built my happiness by taking advantage of others and exploiting their needs. As I looked out my window, I remembered all those days I charged other refugees for every little thing. I even charged them for taking them outside of their rooms. But now I felt like them – even worse than them – because the people who ran the hospital were charging me for the ability to walk again.

Seeing the damage that I had done to my body, I sometimes wondered if I would ever be able to walk or run again. I could not move my leg and hands; my eyes still could not focus, and my vision was dim and weak. I had tubes coming and going everywhere from my body. They put a tube in my head so blood could drip into a bag. And because I was not able to walk to the bathroom, they had to attach a catheter to collect my urine. I thought all this was punishment from God. I was not hurt because I was brave; I was hurt because someone wanted to show me how the world really is: the reality of life is being free to go to the beach and walk next to the sea.

Somewhere along the way I had lost my innocence. I wanted to be free again. To live and to enjoy God's creation had become my only dream.

I stayed in that hospital almost three months. During that time, I became friends with all the doctors and nurses. Everyone knew what happened to me, but they did not know why. I was the only one who knew why all this happened. For a long time, I did not have any visitors, but my other roommates, shared my situation with their friends and they started coming over to visit me. That is why I love Turkey and the Turkish people: they shared their love with me regardless of who I was and where I was from. They loved me and cared about me; they fed me and sometimes, they washed my body because I was not able. I owe a lot to that hospital and those people who came to visit me.

One day a lady came just to visit me and sat down next to me. She started talking to me, gave me her phone and she said I could call my family and talk as long as I wanted. She would pay for the calls. Then she said I could keep the phone and she would get it the day I was released from the hospital. The kindness of this stranger made me cry. I did not know how I could ever thank her as she left the room. It was a great comfort for me to be able to call my family and friends whenever I needed to talk to them.

Not long after that, a friend came to visit me. He told me that my story was shown all over the television news the day I fell and almost died trying to escape the police. He told me I could sue the police and they would pay me for all my injuries and give me citizenship. He said, "Everybody knows you in Turkey. They know your history, but no one knows exactly happened when you were trying to escape from that rooftop." He told me I could make up any story I wanted and sue the police. "Tell the government that the police threw you or pushed you off the roof." But I did not want to make up some story that the police forced me to jump. The truth was I did it to myself. It was enough for me that they left me alone as soon as I started feeling better and will let me go free as soon as I am well enough to leave the hospital.

After three months of treatment, the day came that I was able to walk on my own two feet again. The doctors said they could not keep me in the hospital anymore – if I stayed any longer, I would have to start paying for my care. I agreed that it was time for me to leave. So, I packed up my few belongings and got ready to leave. I walked out of the hospital with no money, one pair of shoes, a phone that did not belong to me, one tee shirt, and shorts. It had been three months since I felt the sun shining on my face. As I started to walk away from the hospital, another stranger came outside and walked beside me. He shook my hand, and when he pulled his hand away, I felt something in the palm of my hand. He had placed fifty Turkish Lira in my hand (about eight U.S. dollars). I was practically speechless; all I could do was say, "Thank you." He told me to "Go. And be careful."

Out on the street, I found the bus station and thought if I went to the section of Istanbul where most refugees lived, maybe I could find some place to stay for a while. I did not realize the terrible shape I was in until I was sitting in the station and the bus came. When I stepped inside the bus, everyone was staring at me. I had lost a lot of weight, my head was not fully healed, and my hand and leg were still wrapped in bandages. I just sat down on the seat in the bus and stared out the windows. I thought about how much of the street scenes I had missed. Before, I almost always took taxis wherever I was going. So, this was only the second or third time I went anywhere in Istanbul on a public bus.

I reached my destination and got off the bus okay, but after a couple of steps, I checked my pocket and realized that I left my phone on the bus on the seat next to me. I tried to get the driver's attention, but my voice was too weak for him to hear. I was too weak, and my injuries meant I could not run after the bus. I could see at that point how helpless and needy I had become. All I could do at that point, was just sit down and cry. A woman was walking towards me. She saw me crying and asked if she could help me. I told her I had lost my phone on the bus. She said, it was no big deal. "I thought you lost your family member or someone dear to you." She did not know that the phone was the only possession I had at that time, and my only lifeline to my friends and family members.

The lady quickly flagged down a taxi for me and paid for it. Then she called my number. The bus driver found my phone and turned it in at the last station on his route. He told me I could go there and pick it up. The taxi driver took me there and I got my phone back. I was so elated the moment I got the phone back in my hands that someone might have thought I found one of my lost body parts. Once again, it was the kindness of a stranger that had saved me.

I had no money, no home, and no one I could call in the city that could help me. I drifted to my old territory in the city, close to the beach. This had once been my kingdom. I had money and people at my command. The refugees I commanded would have to bow down to me if they wanted anything. Now, I was the desperate one. I had totally lost my power and direction. I had lost all the phone numbers of my contacts in and around the city. I would have to call my mom and ask her for money. This was the first time they would have to send money to me from home. And this would be the first time I would have to face the challenge of receiving that money as a poor immigrant in a hostile place.

It took some time, but I did receive the $100 she wired to me. Still, that first night alone was especially hard for me. I walked around my shattered kingdom, alone and cut off from anyone who could help restore me to power. I walked around the beach all day until I was too tired to walk another step. I found a playground and crawled inside one of the big play accessories to sleep. A couple of hours later I heard the voices of a couple of people speaking my native Afghan language. They were talking about their next journey to go to Greece when I crawled out and stood in front of them. At first, they just stared at me, but when I said "hello" they realized I was friendly and meant them no harm.

They had made a fire and invited me to sit down with them. They started asking me questions about what had happened to me. I did not want to tell them the truth, so I made up a story that a car had hit me and ran away. They shared some tea and food with me and we spent a couple of nights together. They told me they had recently been deported from Greece. They lost all their money getting to Greece and now had no place to go. The smuggler that had got all their money was not answering their calls and so now they were left stranded on the beach in Istanbul. I asked the name of the smuggler, and to no surprise, learned it was my old big boss. They were ready to leave and try again to make it to Greece. After they left, I did not hear any news from them; I can only hope they made it all the way.

I stayed alone on the beach for another day. Still not sure what to do or where to go, when I saw a tall, thin man approaching me. He spoke to me in his Turkish language and asked me if I needed a room to stay. I told him yes and asked if he had one to rent. He did not remember me, but I knew his name before he spoke it. His name was Javid and he was known around the area as a drug dealer. But I knew I could not stay outside any longer with no bathroom and no shower. I was getting super dirty, and my body was starting to itch from my wounds. Javid told me it would cost me $100 if I wanted to stay in one of his rooms. It did not matter if I stayed one night or a whole month, the price was the same. I said it was okay with me and he took me inside where I saw a family and a couple of other immigrants staying in the house.

They did not pay much attention to me when I came in. Most were sitting and playing cards, which is one of the favorite pastimes in the Afghan community. While the mother was making food for her family, I quickly settled in. The first thing I wanted to do was take a shower. I had to cover my bandages with plastic bags to keep them from getting wet. It was difficult to achieve, but I managed to clean my body without spoiling my bandages. After I got dressed and joined the others in the house, they started asking me the same questions over and over about what had happened to me. I still did not want to tell anyone the truth about me and so I gave out little or no information about my past. A couple of them told me the story of some Afghan guy who jumped from a building. "It was on all the news." I said, that had heard about it too. I was just trying to distance myself from my recent past life as a smuggler.

From my past experiences, I could see that this house was going to be a problem. It was too visible and the activities of the people who lived there would only draw the attention of the police to the place. So, I was expecting the police to come and find this house sooner or later. I told everyone in the house to be prepared for the police to come, but nobody believed me until it was too late, and the police came knocking at our door. This time, the experience with the police was completely different.

They did not come crashing through the door and threatening everybody. Instead, they were polite and gently handcuffed everybody except me. However, this time the police were not arresting illegal refugees or those violating human trafficking laws. This time, the people being arrested in the house were being arrested on the much more serious charge of selling illegal drugs. As they took people away, I was waiting for my turn for them to come and take me to jail along with them. However, I was surprised by one of the police officers who came towards me and handed me the key to the apartment. He informed me that I could stay there and turned to leave. I just looked at him, too stunned to believe what was happening. He never gave me time to ask him why he did not arrest me with the others, but I suspect it was because my identity and story were well-known by the police and they did not want any more bad publicity by arresting me again.

They took all the other people living in the apartment to the police van. Before being taken away, one of the men staying there turned to me and said they should have listened to me. "It's too late now." Was all I could say to him. After only a few minutes, all were gone, and I was standing there by myself with the key to the apartment in my hand. I was wondering what I was going to do now. I couldn't stay in that apartment all by myself with no money. I hated to call my mother and ask her for more money the first time and I did not want to make it a habit to call her whenever I needed more.

I left the apartment to get some fresh air and to walk and think. I wished I could have walked a little faster when I stepped out onto the street, but I was still sore and bandaged on my leg. Just then, a man stepped in front of me and asked me if I happened to be from Afghanistan. I told him, yes. And he asked me if I knew a place where he and some others with him could stay for the night. They were leaving for Greece in the morning and just needed a place to stay for one night. He told me they were willing to pay. I asked him why he was asking me. And he replied that they could not trust just anybody. But because I was also from Afghanistan, they believed they could trust me.

I told him that I had a place for them to stay and it would cost them $20 per person. They agreed to pay that amount and stayed that night with me.

They were true to their word and the next morning, they were gone before I woke up. So, in one day I made $100. The very day this group left I got a call from a couple of other people. They told me they got my number from Greece and asked if I had a room to rent for one night.

I said I did, and after one week my house was full. My number was quickly being circulated around the network of refugees traveling through Istanbul on their way to Greece.

I was making good money for about a month before the owner of the building came around and told me I had to leave. He said he knew what I was doing in that apartment and he did not want to be a partner to this crime by letting me stay. I told him I understood and grabbed my shoes and some personal items and moved out. By that time, I had two other roommates from Afghanistan staying with me, and they had to leave with me. Once again, I found myself out on the street and no place to go. I remembered that one of the immigrants that passed through my place told me that I should go to the United Nations office in Ankara (The United Nations High Commissioner for Refugees or UNHCR has its headquarters for Turkey in Ankara). He told me that if I gave them my name, they would put me on a list to send me to America or Australia. I decided it was worth the try, so I bought a ticket for Ankara and once again, I left Istanbul behind me. i was there few years ago and ig ot just a paper that showed who i am but i didnot know they will send refugee to other contrys.

CHAPTER FIFTEEN

BECOME A OFFICIAL REFUGEE

The next morning, I was in Ankara and I wasted no time looking for the UNHCR office. After an initial screening, my second interview lasted about two hours. After the second interview, they told me they were going to send me to another city, and I would have to live there. The place they wanted to send me was farther south in Turkey and away from everyone I knew in Istanbul. However, while waiting my interview, I did make friends with a couple other Afghans and as it turned out, they were going to the same city I was assigned to live. They encouraged me to stay with them for a few days until I could find a permanent place to go. At first, I said, "No thanks. I'm going back to Istanbul." But my roommate that came with me to Ankara encouraged me to go to the south. "You don't have a place to stay in Istanbul. Let's go and see what is there. If you don't like it, you can always go back to Istanbul anytime you want."

I agreed and purchased my ticket for the city where we were supposed to go. As planned, we stayed a couple of days at my new friends' house while I searched for a house or apartment I could rent. I found a house; it was old but habitable. Once I settled in, I started to like the new city where we were staying. We stayed there for a couple of months and discovered the house we lived in was close to a big marketplace called the Iranian Bazaar. Although this place is in Turkey, most transactions were made with Iranian currency, and most shop owners were fluent in Farsi, the modern Persian language, which is spoken by some 70 million people mostly from Iran. Anyone who walked into that Bazaar might think they were in Iran. Because we were very close to the place where Syria and Iran borders Turkey, travelers going to Syria to visit Muslim holy places liked to stop and shop here. Iranians know that Turkish jeans are famous for their high quality, but at a cheap price.

After checking everything out, my roommates and I decided to stay for a while, find jobs, and settle there until we could find our way out of Turkey and to the West. There were three of us and we could share expenses, which would make living expenses very cheap. Unfortunately, after a couple of weeks, one of my roommates started playing games with me. He did not want to pay his fair share of expenses. He argued that since he was gone all day and only slept there at night, he did not want to pay. I was very upset with him. And told him, "I helped you come here. You are living at the place I rented. And now you are telling me you don't want to pay me anything?"

I was angry. We started arguing and insulting each other. Our argument quickly evolved into a fistfight. Only a few moments before, we were friends. Now we were wrestling, punching, and biting each other. I stood over him and saw he was lying on the floor with his nose bleeding badly. I had broken his nose in the fight. Our other roommate came in from another room to break up the fight and separate us, but it was too late – the damage had been done. I told my other roommate that I wished he had come sooner, but he said he did not expect this from us. My roommate with the broken nose insisted he was going to call the cops on me even though I promised to pay the medical costs to fix his nose. "But" I said, "if you call the police, don't ask me for anything."

He called the police anyway, and it was not too long before the police showed up at our door. They looked at my roommate, asked us some questions about what had happened, and wrote down their report. After they left, I told my roommate he could not stay with me any longer. He would have to get out immediately and find another place to stay. So, he packed his things and left that night. All night long, I thought about my actions. I kept asking myself why I got so angry, and why I could not control myself before it was too late, and had allowed my anger to end our friendship.

It was not long before I had my own store at the Iranian Bazaar. I opened it with another Afghan friend, and we were making good money. I was going to Istanbul every week to bring goods for the store. Things were going well, but a couple of months later, I got a letter from the municipal court informing me to show up for the trial with my roommate. I tried to find his number, but he had changed it. I did finally find his number and called him to tell him we had to go to court together and to be ready on the day we were supposed to show up. He told me he wanted to meet me before the court day because he had something important to say to me. I agreed to meet him, thinking that he probably wanted to get some money from me or something like that to withdraw his complaint and pull the case out of court.

My ex-roommate came to my house that same night. He knocked on the door, I opened it, and he came in. I reached out my hand to shake his hand, but he grabbed me and hugged me. I was completely taken aback by his action. I did not understand what he was doing or why. We went upstairs where I had some food prepared. I offered him something to eat, but he said no thanks. He came because he had something that he wanted to tell me. I was in suspense and waited for him to tell me what he had come to say. What he said was totally unexpected. He told me that he was going to tell the judge that it was all his fault and ask them to withdraw his complaint against me. I was completely shocked and asked him if he was sure that was what he wanted to do.

I asked him what he wanted from me in return for him taking all the blame for what happened that night. He told me he wanted nothing, but I was suspicious of his motives. After he left, I could not understand why he would do that if there was nothing in it for him. I could not believe him until we had our day in court. We went together to meet with the judge at the court. As promised, he stood before the judge and told him everything was his fault and he wanted to withdraw his complaint against me. The judge told me that he was prepared to give me a sentence of eight months in jail, but after my ex-roommate's testimony, he was not going to sentence me. But if I got in another fight and came to his court, he would certainly send me to jail for eight months. I said that I understood, and we left the courtroom.

As we walked outside, I asked my ex-roommate about that night. I reminded him that he was the one who was insisting to call the police, but today he forgave me. Why? He said, "Do you remember the Afghan guy who was staying with us then? He became a Christian, and I hated him." I said, I remembered. "You were telling me that you don't like this guy because you thought he had sold his Muslim beliefs. You thought he was doing it to get a free home and salary."

So, I asked him, what happened after he left my house that night. He said the night he left, he was out on the streets and did not know where he should go when he received a phone call. It was that Afghan Christian, and he invited him to come to his house. When he got there, it was not just a house, but it was also church. "I started staying there and I am staying there now," my ex-roommate told me. He went on to say that he had a change of mind, and that now he too was a Christian. He told me that the Bible says we should forgive our enemies and do good to those who harmed you. So, he obeyed what his Bible told him and forgave me.

I could see that he had changed a lot and I told him, "The night you came and hugged me, I realized that you had changed, but I did not imagine you changed this much." I reminded him that he used to study at the Mosque, and that he memorized passages from the Quran. "Yes," he said, "but I did not learn anything except revenge, unforgiveness, and hate." But the Afghan Christian he met showed him the God of the Bible is forgiveness and love. Despite all the bad things my ex-roommate said to him and about him, that Christian guy and his family, loved him and opened his house to him. His story had made an impression on me, and after I said goodbye to him, I was thinking all the way home what an amazing story he told me. I wondered how that guy could give him permission to live with him after he had shown such hatred toward him. But before long, I forgot about my ex-roommate and returned to the regular routine of my life.

As the new year approached, my friend and I started cleaning our shop and washing the floors. Turkish people are almost all Muslims, and not many Muslims celebrate the New Year. My friend, Hadem came and visited me at the shop one day. He announced it was Christmas and invited us to come to church for the first time. I told him I had been to church before, but we agreed to come anyway. After he left, we returned home to change clothes and prepared ourselves to go to church for a Christmas celebration.

When I stepped inside that church, I discovered it was totally different than the church I had been to before. We sat in the back of a crowded room. Instead of statues, there were a couple of Scriptures on the walls. As we sat down, the people were singing, and they kept singing worship songs throughout the church service. After the worship was over, we got the opportunity to introduce ourselves. They gave us tea and a cookie. A lady from Iran came up to me and said hello. Before we arrived at the church, my friend told me we should not become friends with any of them because they will only try to convert us. But I started talking with that woman and she gave me an apple to eat. We shared a few friendly words about ourselves and then it was time for my friend and I to leave. As I turned to leave, we shook hands and she invited us to come again, but I remembered my friend's advice and knew she only wanted to convert me. I politely said I would come again but had no plans to return ever.

A couple of days later, my friend Hadem called me and asked me to let him borrow my bank card to get money being sent to him from somewhere. I trusted him and said it would be okay. He came to my shop, grabbed my card and quickly left. I was going to Istanbul to buy some new goods for the shop and needed the card back. So, I called him and asked him to return the card. He was in a meeting and said if I didn't mind coming to him to pick it up, it would be great. I didn't mind. The meeting he was attending was at his church. The church met on the fifth floor of the building. I did not want to go in, so when I arrived, I called him and asked him to throw the card from the window down to where I was standing. He put the card in a bag and threw it out the window, but the wind caught the bag and blew it into an open window on the third floor and it dropped inside the balcony.

Fortunately, Hadem knew the people who lived there; they were from his church. He told me to come up and he would come down and we would meet at their door. When both of us reached the floor, he knocked on the door and I heard a woman's voice speaking Farsi as she came to answer the door. When she opened the door, and I saw her face, I recognized her as the same woman who gave me the apple on the night of the Christmas service. I said hello and we went inside. We explained what had happened, but it must have sounded like a made up story to her at first. She did allow us to search her balcony and I found the card. She said that a couple of days before, she found two pigeons. Both died at the same time, and there were a lot of worms around them, but she just cleaned it up. I thanked her, said goodbye, and left. But as I was walking back to my shop, I could not help but think that there was something more between us. I had the feeling that she was trying to tell me something, but I did not want there to be any misunderstanding about my intentions.

A few days later, I was back from Istanbul and I saw her as I was walking in the city. I don't remember exactly where I was going, but I saw her with her son and her husband. As they came up to me, they said hello. I knew her husband. We worked at the same Bazaar. He had been living in the city for almost fifteen years. After a while, we became friends, but I knew he was addicted to drugs. So, I was careful not to be around people like him too much. He invited me to come to his house the next Friday, and I reluctantly accepted his invite.

I arrived a little early on Friday and my friend was not home yet. I called him and let him know I was waiting for him at his house, but he said I should go inside, and he would be there in about one hour. While I was waiting for him, his son came and started talking to me. He was a cute little boy. He had a new dog and was excited to show him to me. I told his mother I was very good at training dogs and if they needed help to train it, I would be happy to do it. As I continued my visit, she started telling me her life story. She shared with me how life was hard for her and how she was struggling raising her son. She was crying and telling me about how miserable her married life had become. Then she told me that she wanted a divorce.

I was totally unprepared to hear her confessions about her marriage. All I could do was sit there and listen as she told me about her husband, my friend. She told me he did not love her or his son. He did not help them or spend time with them. She told me that in the four years they had been living there, he had never taken his son to the park to play. "I am constantly finding drugs in his pocket and in the kitchen." He kept denying the drugs were his, but it was obvious to her that they belonged to him and that he had become totally addicted to drugs. I did not want to interfere with her marriage or come between the two of them, but in my mind, I knew what she was saying was true. I knew a lot more about her husband than she was aware of, but I could not speak of those things to her.

When he finally did come home, we sat down together and ate dinner as if nothing had been said between his wife and me. I had a small gift for their son and gave it to him. I told my friend that it was time for me to go, but he insisted that I stay the night. I told him, no and that I must be going. But again, he insisted that I stay with them overnight. Again, I said no, I had to go. After insisting a third time that I stay, I said okay. After I said I would stay, he disappeared into another room. I don't know what he was doing there, but he never came back out to talk to me again that night. I thought that maybe he just wanted me to stay and spend time with his son. He just left me alone his wife, Jeyran, and his son. After a couple of hours, she showed me a room where I could lay down and sleep.

It was the middle of the night and I was asleep when suddenly I heard screaming and yelling coming from outside my bedroom door. At first, I thought that something had happened to their son, but soon figured out that my friend and his wife were fighting. He was yelling at her and insulting her. I knew that a domestic dispute between husband and wife was none my business and I should stay out of it. So, I just stayed in my room and tried to go back to sleep. I stayed until the morning and left without saying anything to either of them.

All that day, I was thinking about them and debating with myself about what I should do. Part of me said I should stay out of it and just let them live their lives. It was not any of my business. But another part of me could not let me ignore the things I saw and the words I heard. In the end, I knew I was not the kind of person who could do nothing when I saw the desperate situation this woman and her son were in. So, I called her and asked her to let me take her and her son to the best park in the city. I told her I wanted to spend time with her son and talk to her about her situation. We walked, sat and talked for almost three hours and then on the way back from the park, I told her I had decided to help her. She stopped, looked at me, and asked me how I could help her situation.

I told her that I was going to hire a lawyer for her to get a divorce. I would also rent a home for her and her son to live together until the divorce was final. "It may take a long time," I said, "but I know you are ready for this." Yes, her husband was a friend, but I could not ignore the way he was destroying their lives. I encouraged her to think about her life and the life of her little boy. If her husband wanted to waste his life on drugs and other self-destructive behavior, that was one thing, but I did not want to see her waste her life and the life of her innocent young child because of him. "I'm going to help you." I said, "I'm in it." She was very happy when we parted. She told me she would call me when she got home. After thirty minutes, she called me and told me, "I'm ready to leave." I said that was too fast. I needed time to find a house for her, but I promised I would start looking the next day.

The next day I found a house for rent. It looked perfect, like someone had made it ready just for her and her son. I called her and told her to grab whatever she had and come to the address I gave her. She arrived in a taxi and stayed at the new apartment that night. The next morning, I was very nervous and stressed out. I wasn't sure if I was doing the right thing or not. Was I saving her life and the life of her son, or destroying the life someone else? But it was too late now, I thought. The decision was made, and things were set in motion that could not be reversed.

We went shopping and I bought whatever they needed for the house. We were living in a small city and every day we saw someone we knew. From the first day, my friends started seeing me with Jeyran. And in a few hours, all my friends and acquaintances were gossiping and messaging about me. I must have received a hundred calls asking me what was going on and asking who this woman was that I was with. At first, I said that she was only a friend and that I was trying to help her out. But it was not long before I faced the truth that I wanted more than to help her as a friend.

I was going through all this because I wanted to marry her. I told Jeyran that as soon as her divorce was final, I wanted to marry her. She could not believe it at first, but I assured her that I was telling her the truth and told her again, "Yes, I will marry you."

CHAPTER SIXTEEN

FINDING MY LIFE PARTNER

I hired a lawyer and we got the divorce process started. Jeyran insisted that as soon as her husband was notified and papers were filed, I should tell him that I was helping her get the divorce. I was against telling him because I was afraid it would complicate things for both of us if he knew I was involved. One day, I was at my store when he came walking in. I was surprised and scared when I first saw him, but I just kept watching him without saying anything. I thought that maybe he knows about me and Jeyran, but he came to me only to borrow some money. He lied to me and said he needed the money for Jeyran because she needed to buy something right away. I asked what it was she needed, but he did not say. Of course, I knew

Jeyran did not ask because she was not living with him anymore. But I gave him the money anyway. I knew he wanted to buy more drugs. However, I thought it best not to say no to him.

I saw him again a couple of days later. He lied to me again and told me that Jeyran said thanks for the money and told me a story about how she needed it. That evening I told Jeyran that it was time for me to tell him the truth about us. I did not want him to come to me for drug money and lie to me, using her as his alibi. She agreed we should tell him. I called him and asked him to meet me at a restaurant. Jeyran and I went together and when he saw us together, he went totally crazy. He started screaming and yelling at her, but I told him to be quiet and calm down so we could talk to him. He jumped to the conclusion that I was encouraging Jeyran to divorce him, but I tried to tell him that she had made up her mind to divorce him before she met me. I was only trying to help her because he was not taking any responsibility to be a good husband and father. But he refused to listen and kept making a disturbance at the restaurant. He was threatening to call the police when the restaurant owner came to our table and asked us to leave his establishment because we were disturbing his other customers. The arguing and yelling continued when we went outside. He was becoming hysterical and ran down the street to a bridge where he threated to throw himself down and kill himself if Jeyran did not agree to come back to him. I knew he was just being overdramatic and told Jeyran we should go and leave him alone until he calmed down. I called a taxi and he just stood there and watched us as we left.

After that meeting, he started harassing Jeyran with phone calls and texts. He threatened her, he called her family and told her mother that she had been cheating on their marriage and ran away with an Afghan boy. She proclaimed her innocence to her husband and her family, but none of her words convinced them of the truth. We knew that it was hard for people to believe us because of the way we had come together and how we were handling the divorce. This was not the normal way a divorce and remarriage happened, and as much as we tried to convince them that we did not have an affair and I did not talk to her about getting married before Jeyran was already set in her mind to divorce him, no one was convinced that we were telling the truth.

Jeyran believed that God had told her some time before she met me that He was going to change her life. "He promised me." She believed the two dead pigeons on her balcony and my credit card ending up on that same balcony were signs from God that a change was about to happen. She believed that God led her to a verse from the Bible (Joel 2:25) that promised God would restore to her "the years that the swarming locusts has eaten." She kept reading that verse to me, but in my heart, I did not believe those things, especially from the Bible. I only agreed with her to make her happy. Because I was not a believer, it was hard for me to understand all the things she was telling me about our meeting being a divine appointment and God's will for her. I had never known a person who talked about God's intervention in their life the way Jeyran did. I still believed that whatever I did in my life – right or wrong – was my decision alone, and nobody else helped me or took responsibility for any of my actions.

Her husband warned Jeyran that he was not going to forget about her. He was not going to sit back and accept the fact that she wanted a divorce. He knew that it was Jeyran that did not want to live with him, but before I came into the picture, he told his brother and other family members that he was the one who sent her away. He told them he wanted to punish her and show her how hard it is to live without him. After she learned her lesson, she would return and beg him to take her back.

It was obvious that the drugs had affected his mind and his ability to see things the way they really were. His behavior changed when he saw me with Jeyran. He finally realized she was not coming back to him, would never beg him to take her back. He tried to bully, beg, plead, threaten, and manipulate Jeyran with words to make her come back to him. He would do anything but promise to give up his drugs, or change any of his behaviors that were the cause of all his personal and marital problems. He was still in denial and blaming her and me for what he had done to his life, his family, and his own son. All he could think about was how he could take revenge on Jeyran.

Night after night when I went to visit Jeyran, she was crying and told me some new thing he had said or done to upset her and make her feel miserable. I told her she needed to just turn off her phone and not talk to him anymore. But she said, I cannot ignore him. We are still married, and he wants to talk to his son. One day I came to check on her and make sure everything was alright. When I saw her, she had collapsed on the kitchen floor. She was so upset and had been crying so much that she was in a terrible emotional state.

I picked up the phone and called her husband to tell him enough is enough, and to leave us alone. He answered the phone and we started arguing. He made me so upset that I hit my fist through a glass widow and cut my hand. There was blood everywhere, but I did not care. I told him to wait at his store because I was coming to talk to him. I walked almost thirty minutes with a bloody hand. I was blind with rage and did not think about anything except that I wanted to see him and settle this trouble with him once and for all time. When I got to his store, he was not there. I called him, but he did not answer the phone. So, I went back to my home and asked my friends to take me to the hospital. My head was spinning, and I was still very angry. I believe if I had seen him, I could have killed him. Once I finally calmed down, I realized that it would be best if I did not see him. I did not want to be involved in another fight that ended in a court case. They put some stiches in my wrist, and I returned home.

I called Jeyran. She was worried about me, but I told her I was alright and not to worry. I insisted that she not talk to her husband anymore. I could not stand another day of this drama with him. If he kept upsetting her, I could not be responsible for my actions toward him. She promised she would not take any more of his calls. We would just have to be patient and wait until the divorce case was final. Not long after this, he called me and asked me to bring their son Ali to visit him. I was suspicious of his motives because he had never been that kind of father. But because Ali was his son, I felt we would have to take him because his father had the right to see him.

I talked it over with Jeyran and we all went to the park to meet him. It was nighttime, and I sat and watched them go over to his father. I was watching to make sure that the visit was going well, but it was not. Almost immediately they started arguing and he grabbed Ali and started to run away. I jumped up and ran to catch up with him and took hold of Ali's arm. Ali became a rope between his father and me. At first, we were pulling him between us, and then we started fighting and biting each other. At that moment a police car pulled up to us and they ordered us to stop fighting. When they asked us to explain what was going on, Ali's father started lying to the police and told them I was trying to steal his wife and son. He said I was trying to keep him from seeing his son. I let him finish his story, and then I pulled out a copy of all the paperwork that our lawyer had filed with the court. I told the officer that his wife had requested the divorce and she no longer lived with him. After the police officer looked over the documents, he turned to Jeyran's husband and rebuked him. He told him that he was in the wrong and should not tell lies about what was happening. I sighed in relief that the police could see what was really happening. Then they asked Ali's father if he was paying any child support. He did not answer, but just turned around and ran away from the police.

The officer told us that they would find him and said we could go. I was relieved that the police were on our side and told Jeyran, "Let's go home." He did not want to see his son; he only wanted to make more trouble for us. All his actions proved that he did not want to change his ways or see Jeyran live free from his problems. On the way back home, I saw a black car pull in front of me. Three rough looking guys stepped out of the car and faced me. One of them pull out a gun and told me to let Jeyran go back to her husband or else they will kill me. They told me to leave the city and don't come back. Then they got back into their car and drove off.

I did not know what they thought I would say. Did they really think that I would leave Jeyran and just flee the city? I knew I was not going to do that. I was going to stay and fight if necessary, but I was worried about Jeyran and Ali; they might come one day when I was not around and hurt them. What if I was not able to protect them as I promised? When we got home, we were discussing what we should do. In fact, my business was down at that time anyway. Another war had started in Syria and Iranians had stopped going to Syria. That meant my business and all the businesses in the Iranian Bazaar were suffering. I suggested to Jeyran that we shift to Istanbul because we would have little or no income if we stayed where we were.

I had a lot of friends in Istanbul. I knew we could make a better living there, and it was no longer safe for us to remain in the city where Jeyran's husband lived. Maybe we could flee to another country. I told her I could take her to Greece or Italy. I knew how to get to those places, but it was just an idea and not something we had to do. I had lost 35 pounds since all this trouble with Jeyran's husband started. Nobody could believe what had happened to me in such a short time. My friends thought I was crazy for putting myself through all that trouble. But they could not feel what I was feeling, and they could not understand that something was pushing me forward and giving me strength. It was a very dangerous stretch, but every time I started to doubt if what I was doing was right, something in my heart kept telling me that nothing bad would happen to me and everything was going to be alright. But nobody else understood that.

Jeyran and I decided to leave the city and started to pack everything. We had been to court twice for her divorce and he refused both times to put his signature on the papers. We were scheduled for a third appearance just before we planned to make our move. I thought he would never let her go and told her it would be a waste of time to go there a third time. But something happened just before the last court date. He called me and said he was coming to sign and let her go. He said he was worn out and exhausted from all the battles, and so were we. He could see that Jeyran's mind was made up, and it was time to put all of this behind him. At first, I did not believe him. He had thrown up so many roadblocks before and had tried everything he could to prevent Jeyran and me from moving on with our lives, but I had no choice except to believe him this last time.

On the day we showed up for court, I did not go inside with Jeyran. I stayed outside because I thought if her husband saw me, he would feel jealous and get crazy again. After almost one hour, Jeyran came out and she was crying. I held her and asked her what happened. She looked into my eyes and she said, "It is done Mehdi. I am free now." I jumped and shouted for joy. We were both so happy because now it meant we could finally get married. We went home from the court and picked up Ali from kindergarten. We decided to celebrate that night and I invited all my friends to come and celebrate with us.

Jeyran had been through a very difficult time. Her family rejected her because of the divorce and did not want to talk to her. Her church rejected her because of the divorce and did not allow her to come to worship services. One of the pastors was telling her to leave me and return to her husband because the Bible strictly prohibits divorce. But Jeyran was a praying person, and she prayed every day, believing that God is not just in church, but he is everywhere. She prayed every morning for one hour and sought God for the strength and courage to carry on with what she believed He wanted for her. She just could not believe that God wanted her to stay in an abusive marriage with a man who was a drug addict and refused to care for his family. She believed God made the way for her to escape from that horrible life, and she should not go back after He opened the door for her to take her child and leave.

After a couple of days, we went to the office to make our intention to marry official. She had to pass a pregnancy test, and I had to bring a paper from the Afghanistan Embassy to show I was single. We brought those things with us and all went well. We signed the necessary papers. There was a waiting period of two months before we could marry, but the day finally arrived. Jeyran was able to go get her haircut and we dressed for our wedding pictures. I had never thought I would dress like a groom, but it was happening. We went alone to register our marriage. We got the marriage certificate in our hands and at last we could be together as husband and wife.

For our honeymoon we went to Izmir, a very nice, beautiful beach city and we spent a couple of days there. We were able to shake off a little of the stressful days, weeks, and months we endured to reach this point. It had been a very troubling time for both of us and our families. Before it was all over, everybody had gotten involved, but the journey had come to an end, and now we looked forward to a new adventure as husband and wife. After we returned from the honeymoon, we came back to our city and started to settle into a normal life. We were officially married now, but we still had another problem: we were both immigrants registered with the United Nations, but our cases were separate. Because our cases were separate, they informed us that even though we were married it could take up to two years to merge us into one case. I did not understand why it took so long. It created a big problem for us because the UNHCR did not recognize us as a family. If anything happened, they would separate us from each other.

We were desperate and exhausted from years of one legal entanglement after another. I did not know what we needed to do next. We had dealt with one problem after another, but there were still more problems ahead of us. We were not doing well emotionally because of all the stress. I wanted to bring my family from Iran so they could visit me. However, this was another big problem because they would have to come illegally, and I did not know if they could make the difficult journey on the same immigrant trail that I followed to reach Turkey. I was still in contact with a lot of good people who could bring my family along the best possible route, and I was ready to pay them. However, even on the best possible route, there were no guarantees that they would survive the journey. Anything was possible, but I had to take that risk, and told my family to come even though I knew all the problems and dangers they would have to overcome.

I was sad to hear that my dad was too sick to come. He told me he could not walk long distances over rough terrain. So, my mom and two sisters came without him. Fortunately, they came easily and without any major problems. I realized that my mom was a very brave woman and must really love me to take such a huge risk to come and see me. At first, we were very happy. After they arrived, we all stayed at the same home. Having my family near us would help us to forget all the pain we had gone through. But after a couple of weeks, other problems came up. We had been making plans for all of us to immigrate to the West, but it was clear that my family would not be allowed to immigrate with Jeyran. Her case was much further along than mine and she would probably be allowed to immigrate long before me. I wanted to be with both of my families and was constantly looking for other options. But it seemed the best option would be to let Jeyran go, and I would have to go later. Otherwise, we would all have to stay in Turkey maybe forever.

One day, we received a call from the American Embassy, and they announced the news that Jeyran and Ali could go to America. I was happy from one perspective, but from another I was not. I was confused and did not know what to do. It was very hard to put my family on a plane and let them go. I did not know how I would be able to do it. I did not know who to trust or who would take care of them in America. I did not know anyone in America that I could call and ask to help them there. All I had were questions and no answers. But we knew all the problems we would have staying here and doubted we could survive indefinitely as illegal refugees in a foreign country. A couple of weeks after receiving the call from the U.S. Embassy, Jeyran and I got an appointment to talk to them and ask them to accept me as her husband, but there was no hope. They told us that Jeyran would have to be separated from me. Once she was in the United States, she could invite me to come, but it could take another two years before I would be able to join them.

By this time, Jeyran was pregnant with our daughter. I was thinking that if it took as long as they said, my daughter would walk and talk without me being there to see her. It was so unfair that I could not see my daughter, my wife, and step-son Ali for two years. I was asking myself, "Why me? Why is everything such a big challenge for me?"

For the two years I lived in Turkey, I never had money problems, but now my business was down, and I did not have enough income to support both of my families. The immigration worries and now the financial troubles were making my life miserable. But Jeyran kept telling me that she was praying to God and He told her to go, and He would help us. I told her, "If God wanted to help us, why is He not helping me now? Why can't I come with you? Why does He not talk to me?"

CHAPTER SEVENTEEN

HARDEST DESICION IN MY LIFE

A couple of more days passed, and we received another call from the Embassy. They wanted a final answer from us. Yes or no; was Jeyran and Ali going to the U.S.? We had only one hour to decide. Jeyran could either go with Ali and send me an invitation or stay here and continue to deal with all the problems. We were still talking and had not reached a final decision when the phone rang again. Both of our hearts were beating fast and neither of us had the courage to say yes, but we both knew there was only right answer. We should not let go of this opportunity to immigrate to America. If we said, "no" now, the chance to go might not come again for years. When the U.S.

Embassy called back, we said "yes" to their call. They gave us a hospital address near the American Embassy at Ankara and asked us to go there and check with the doctor to see if Jeyran was able to fly. In my heart, I hoped the doctor would say "no" and she could stay here, but I would not know until I got her to the hospital. I had heard from friends that if Jeyran was more than eight months pregnant, she could not fly. So, I was tense all day long. We arrived at the hospital a little early for her appointment. Jeyran was told by the doctor not to eat anything before the examination. I didn't want to eat anything either. So, we were both hungry and anxious while we sat in the waiting room. When it was time, the doctor called Jeyran to come into the examination room while I had to wait outside. A few minutes later, Jeyran came out and she was crying. I did not know what had happened and was afraid to ask. But as I opened my mouth to ask, she told me the doctor told her I could go with no problem. I had hoped that Jeyran and Ali would come back with me and we could all stay, but I had to face the fact that they would go, and I would have to stay behind without them.

The doctor came out and said, "Congratulations, your wife can fly." and told me that he was sending a fax to the Embassy. I told him that this was not something I can celebrate and be happy about. I was full of sorrow. This doctor was thinking like so many others that when anyone gets permission to go to America, they were happy. But I was different because I was disappointed and sad that it would mean our family was being torn apart. I was speechless on the bus ride home. We hugged each other and did not say a word for the entire ten hour journey home. Ali was asleep on the floor under the seat. Jeyran and I were lost in our thoughts, just wondering about what the future was going to be.

After we got back home, we made ready all the final provisions for their departure. We packed their suitcases and were prepared when they called us and told us the plane tickets were ready. They gave us the exact date and time of the flight. The days were passing faster than before, and we could not hold on to them. Jeyran and Ali were ready to go, but we all knew the last day was going to be a hard day for all of us. Our final moments at the airport was the hardest time of my life. We were crying and Jeyran was not able to walk. They brought a wheelchair, and someone had to push her. She needed my help, but I was not allowed to pass the security checkpoint. They took her and Ali behind those black blinds and we just looked at each other. She was crying, and I was crying. I did not want to be apart from her for even one second. But then someone came and pushed her wheelchair and she was out of my sight and being taken from me. He did not know it, but he was pushing my heart from my body. Every step they were taking was hurting me more. Every minute she was going farther and farther from me. I could not stand it that I could no longer see her.

I ran around to see if I could find a place to watch her. I was lifting my head above everyone, hoping that maybe I could see her one last time. If I could only just say to her one last time, "Bye, honey. I will come. I promise." But I could not see her. She was gone. I sat down in the airport and I was thinking, "Mehdi, they are gone. What am I doing here? What will happen to them? Who will help them?" A thousand questions were going through my mind. Jeyran's airplane took off, and I had to leave the airport. I just stood there, looking into the sky, thinking maybe I can see her or maybe she can see me standing and looking for her.

This was the second time in my life that America was taking away a loved one. First, America took my childhood friend, Give, and now it was taking my wife, my baby, and my son. I did not understand why it did this to me. "What did I do to you, America that you turned my life into darkness?" They called America a blessed country, but for me, I hated it for what it had done to me.

The first night alone, I could not sleep. I was holding my phone, waiting for them to call me. I did not want to miss their call, telling me they arrived safely. They promised to call me right away, but I did not receive a call for almost four days and three nights. I was going crazy and calling everywhere I could think of. I called the Embassy, the hospital, and any place I could call, but there was no answer. Finally, after four days, I received a call from Jeyran. I could feel the pain in her voice. She was tired and she told me that night she arrived, she stated bleeding. They rushed her to the hospital and Ali was staying in another family's house. We did not know who that other family was, but we had no other option. She was crying and I was trying to give her strength and hope. But I did not have any of my own to give her. How could I give her something I did not have? We were both tired and depressed. It was so hard to live in this situation. But we had no other choice now. It was extremely difficult for a man like me to not have a hand in determining the outcome of my fate. I knew that my family needed help, but I was far away and could not do a thing for them. It made me more frustrated and angrier but what could I do?

They released Jeyran from the hospital and sent her home. She was doing well and so was the baby. They gave her a small one bedroom apartment and she needed to take care of herself and Ali. But I was afraid that she could not do it all alone. They had promised me that they would take care of her needs, but they were doing nothing. After two weeks she did not even have a telephone. Every time I wanted to talk to her I had to call her neighbor. It was almost time for our daughter to be born and I was happy she will be born in America, but I am sad that I cannot be there when she is born. I would not be able to see her and did not know when I would be able to take her in my hands and look into her eyes. I could only image how sweet she will be and hope I would see her one day.

A couple of days went by and I did not have a chance to talk to Jeyran. No one answered my phone calls and I was very worried that something was wrong. Not knowing what was going on only increased my tension. Finally, Jeyran's neighbor answered the phone. I asked him what was happening, and he did not say anything. I knew something was not right when he said he was passing the phone to Jeyran. I was sweating and my heart was pounding. Breathlessly, I waited for Jeyran's voice to tell me the bad news. Had something happened to Jeyran? Or to my daughter? Or to Ali? I thought, "O God, please help me." When Jeyran came on the phone, I could barely hear her voice. She could not talk very well. She told me she caught chicken pox. She could not talk or eat and was not feeling good at all. "O my God," I said, "Where did this come from, Jeyran? Where is Ali?"

Ali was visiting in a neighbor's house. He got the chicken pox and before Jeyran knew it, Ali had passed it on to her. I called for an ambulance a couple of times, but they said because of my sickness, they could not take me to the hospital. Chicken pox is highly contagious, and they were afraid that other moms and their kids might be exposed to it and catch it from me. I said, "Really? This is America? They left you like that, and they promised me that they would take care of you. They have all the technology, but they cannot protect my wife and daughter?" She was unable to talk and passed the phone to the neighbor. I asked him to please tell me what was going on. He said that because she has chicken pox, they cannot admit her into a hospital. She needed to get better. She was not good at all now because it got into her mouth and she cannot eat food or talk.

I was crying over the phone and I sat down, not knowing what to do. I prayed, "They need help, God, where are You? Where are Your promises? Everybody promised me, but nobody kept them. You are doing the same thing. You don't keep Your promise." I remembered my mom told me a couple of days before Jeyran and Ali left, she had a dream and she saw me with two pigeons in my two hands and another person standing beside me, asking me to release them and let them go. And I did. My mom believed in her dreams and that they would come true. So did I. She said that the dream was a message from God. That I needed to let them go. Jeyran said the same thing. She prayed every day and she told me God put a peace in her heart and asked her to go. But I had my doubts if God really spoke to my mom and my wife that He would take care of them. Why was all this happening to my family? I did not have any answers. I could only wait to see what would happen next.

I was calling constantly to find out what was happening and if they were going to take Jeyran to the hospital or not. Finally, they did take her to the hospital and after a week the sickness passed. She was still very weak and was not able to talk. She had not been able to eat very much and had lost a lot of strength and blood too. She was well enough to go back home, and the doctors gave her another appointment to go back to the hospital on the baby's due date. I was excited and afraid, not knowing if something would go wrong with Jeyran or if the baby would be born healthy.

It was at this time that an Iranian church near Jeyran found out that there was an Iranian lady who immigrated from Turkey who needed help. Thank God for them because they came to Jeyran's rescue. They rented another apartment for Jeyran closer to the church and people from the church started taking care of her. I did not talk to any of them at the time, but I hoped that one day I would see them and tell them thank you.

The due date came and people from the church took Ali with them and took Jeyran to the hospital to give birth to our daughter. I was so nervous and did not know what I could do but just wait, hold my breath, and ask God to help them. There was no one to help me and I was alone as I waited for news. I realized then that in some situations in life, whether you are alone or if someone is with you, the only one who can help is God Himself. But I did not know how to pray. Jeyran was always telling me to pray and God would listen, but I was not believing. In my religion, there was no prayer like this. We memorized all our prayers and read them in Arabic. I didn't know exactly what they meant, but I said them because that is what we are supposed to do. But Jeyran had a different meaning to prayer. She told me to say in my own words what I wanted to say to God, and He would listen to me and answer me. I thought, now I can try at least, but I did not know how.

I wanted to be there with Jeyran. I knew I should have been there with her. I should hold her hand and give her confidence as her husband. I should look into her eyes and give her strength, but I could not even talk to her. I was sitting in my store, and looking around as customers were coming in, but I was not paying attention to them. I decided to close the door and turn off the lights. Then I sat down and put my hands together to pray. I said to myself and God, "If you hear me, if you are real, and you told me to send them, then please protect my family. Please. Amen."

It was almost afternoon before I got a call from one of the doctors. She got my Skype ID from Jeyran and called me. She told me that my daughter was born, but they had to put her into an incubator because she had a problem with her heart. I said, "What do you mean? Show me my daughter. Is she okay? Is Jeyran okay?" The doctor told me that Jeyran was okay. She was still unconscious, and I would have to wait until she woke up before I could talk to her. She turned off the Skype and I was still sitting in my store waiting when I got a call from one of the Iranian ladies from the church. She told me that Jeyran was okay and my daughter would be okay too. I asked her why they put her in another room, but she said not to worry, she was sure my daughter would be okay. After talking to her, I was relieved and could finally take a deep breath and relax. I would have to wait for Jeyran to wake up before I could talk to her and feel better.

Jeyran was released from the hospital, but they wanted to keep our daughter there until they were confident that she was out of danger. Jeyran was still in pain from the surgery and emotionally, she was longing to be able to hug and nurture her newborn baby. She had carried her in her womb for nine months, waiting to see this moment, but she had to wait. We were both crying, but there was nothing I could do to help either of us forget the emotional pain. For a couple of days, Jeyran had to use a breast pump and take her milk to the hospital to feed the baby. All my family was under stress as we waited for some good news about my daughter. I must give many thanks for those who helped Jeyran with transportation to and from the hospital. They were awesome people. I had never known people like them. They were so kind to help.

Fortunately, this situation did not last long. After a few days, we got the good news. They told

Jeyran to come and hug your child and you can take her home. She is well and healthy now. This was a joyful and unforgettable day for us. Jeyran called me and she had our daughter in her hands. She was kissing her and holding her. The moment I saw her face on the small screen on my phone, I gave thanks to God for this beautiful baby girl. I thought she was so beautiful. I could not believe that this was my daughter. What I had done to deserve this? I only wished I could be there to hug and kiss her and hold her in my arms. But I would have to wait. At least she was safe in her mother's arms and she was okay. I could see my daughter sleeping quietly. She did not have any stress like us. She did not know anything about our problems, and she was relaxed, knowing she is in good hands that were committed to protect her and save her the best way they could. I wished I could be like her. Who is my savior? Who is the one committed to protect me and my family in this wild world? Who do I call when I need to be held? I did not know. I did not know. I had no answers. I felt really lost.

CHAPTER EIGHTEEN

BECOME A FATHER

Shortly after my daughter was born, I received a notice from the government that they were planning a new highway and had I ten days to vacate. I did not have enough time or money to relocate my shop, so I was forced to close it. I quickly emptied out my store, but I did not know what I was going to do next. Jeyran needed money. I did not have a penny to feed myself and take care of my family. All my money was gone. I remembered the days when I made thousands of dollars. I could make as much as forty thousand dollars in one night as a human smuggler, but now I did not have a penny. The old saying, "Easy come... Easy go..." had become real for me.

I was looking for a job when got a call from one of my friends. He bought a truck and said we could make money recycling cardboard and plastic from trashcans. I did not have any other job prospects, so I decided to join him. We started collecting cardboard boxes and plastic bottles and containers from around the city and selling them for recycling. We worked long days and the work was dirty. We had to dig through nasty trash to find some boxes and pull them out. At the end of each day we might make only a couple hundred Turkish lira – just enough to feed ourselves and pay the rent. But that was all I could do. As I traveled in and around the city all day long looking for boxes, I was thinking "What happened to me rising? Now I'm down in the dirt and filth." I could not believe the situation I was in. It was unbelievable what life had become. But it was not a nightmare – it was real. At one time, I was living like a king, but now I could not buy food for myself. When was this was going to end? I did not know, but I had to stay. There was no escape for me.

Escape was always the solution for me before. I was always looking for the next place that I could run to and get away from whatever problems I had.

This is who I had become – a runner. Now I had to learn this big lesson that sometimes there is no way you can get away from your problems. You have no choice but to stay and fight it out. So, every day I would work hard and coming back home at night I could smell the garbage that stuck to my clothes and my body. My hands were dirty, my clothes were torn, and I smelled like trash. One day I saw a family living inside a trash container. They had ten children, and their only toys were the ones they scavenged from trashcans. But they seemed happy. They were like the birds of the air or the lilies of the field, living day-to-day with no worries about the future and no stress about the present. Collecting trash, I encountered people living another lifestyle I had never thought about before. It opened my eyes to another facet of life, and I could see more than my own troubles and feel the pain that others felt.

In my spare time I learned the art of carving watermelons. I enjoyed it and had a knack for it. Everyone who saw my carvings told me I was talented and could become highly skilled. One day, I was watching TV and I saw a Turkey's Got Talent TV show. They announced they were coming to my city looking for new talents and I thought I would go and register. "Who knows, maybe I can go from trash can to TV show." I saw this happen in America. Average people got on TV and became famous for their voice or whatever. So, I applied and the day they came for me to audition for their show. I cut my first watermelon for them. It was a very basic design I did for them. They told me to go home and they would call me. I thought they did not like it and they would never call me again, but a couple days later I received a text message from the producers inviting me to be on their show.

I was very surprised and could not believe that I was going to be on TV. It was so surreal. I was going from wading through garbage to being on TV. I practiced and prepared myself for the show. When the day came and they announced my name to go on stage, I went in front of almost 4,000 university students that filled the hall from where the show was being broadcast. It was the largest crowd I had seen in my life in one place. Before I got to the show, I talked to Jeyran and she was happy for me. I asked her to watch me while I was on stage. I performed in front of a famous, wealthy man in Turkey. He was an incredible man – humble and polite to me. I did a great job, and everyone liked my carving. I got a positive response from everyone and big applause from the crowded hall.

Overnight, I became famous. I got 5,000 new followers on my Facebook page and every day, people kept adding me and sending me new friends requests. It quickly reached a point where I could not lift my head from the computer because of the number of messages I received from people all around the world. They liked my performance and it was a great feeling being appreciated for my talent. Like so many other children, I had this dream that I would be famous and rich. Now, I felt I was going to get rich the right way. I cannot explain the feeling, but it was amazing. Even though I did not want to be puffed up, fame can make a person proud and make them walk around with chest up. I never thought I would be someone people would walk up to and ask to take their picture with, or someone that strangers wanted my autograph. I called Jeyran and she was happy to see me. She told me that she watched me with the children, and they all enjoyed it. It was one moment at least that we could forget some of our problems and renew our lost hope for a better future.

Jeyran told me she did not want to stay in California. She spoke with some of her relatives that had a big house in Georgia, and she wanted to move there. I did not understand why she was insisting to move, but a couple of days later, she called me from her relative's house in Georgia. My TV appearance paid me enough, so I did not have to work collecting trash every day. That was important to me. I was able to pass the second and third rounds on the show. When I got to the final round of Turkey's Got Talent show, it was a big dream coming true for me. I was working with watermelon every day now, but after being a TV celebrity for a couple of months, I started to feel uncomfortable about being famous. Some people were jealous of me and started making fun of me. Some people tried to ruin my reputation by spreading false rumors about my life and character. I knew that not everyone had to like me, but I started feeling guilty about being a celebrity to people who knew me. I could understand why big celebrities wanted to hide themselves from people. I always thought they were crazy. I thought everyone wanted to be famous, but why did they hide themselves from their fans? The first thing I learned from being on that TV show was that being famous was not really that big of a blessing. Sometimes it is a bigger problem.

I started hating my new names and strangers kept bothering me, asking weird questions about my income and asking a lot of different things about my personal life. It had been my dream to become famous, but once I achieved some fame, I no longer wanted it. On the final TV show, I did not do a good job. Everything was messed up. After that, I could not go on the street because of the way people reacted to me after I failed to meet their expectations. I tried not to listen to the bad things people were saying about me, but I felt like there was no place to hide. After my final TV appearance, it did not take very long for my life to get back to normal. I got an offer from a large and celebrated restaurant that needed a chef. I was happy to accept their offer. It was a busy place with a lot of customers. A couple of other Afghans were working there too, and I was made head over them and all the other kitchen staff.

So, in the end, the TV show helped me to get a little extra money. I worked there almost a year and enjoyed it. But the whole time I was missing my family. Even though I was talking with Jeyran every night from Skype, I missed them terribly. I was watching Ali and Radmila growing from afar and wondered if Radmila knew who I was. Jeyran told me she was having a problem with the family. They changed their minds and they did not want her and the children living with them anymore. When I asked why, she said that our kids and their kids kept fighting – especially Ali. They did not want any more fighting. So, they asked them to leave as soon as possible. I asked her where she wanted to go. I could not send her any money at that time because I made barely enough to pay my rent and buy food for my family. She told me she was praying and was sure God would provide her with everything they needed. Although I still had my doubts, I agreed and told her, "Yes, He will, I'm sure."

She used her phone to show me all around her room. She put a lot of prayer notes on her walls and kept reading her Bible every day. I wished I had faith like hers, but I did not. I remembered I did everything for myself since I was a child and I did not ask anybody, even my father, for help. I learned that I needed to take action to find a job and work hard if I wanted to be a success. But Jeyran quoted a verse from the Bible that said, "And we know that in all things God works for the good of those who love him, who have been called according to his purpose." It was good and I liked the sound of it, but I did not believe or trust God enough to live by it. In my personal life I could not see any place where God helped me. I thought I did everything by myself.

One day Jeyran called me and said God answered her prayers and she found a place. There was a lady living alone who needed help paying rent and utility bills and she was going to move into her basement. I was happy to hear that she found a church that helped her move and helped with all her expenses. I was very grateful for those people who were helping my wife and children. I was tired of being separated from my family and wondering how much longer I had to live like this. I started thinking that maybe I should divorce her and let her live in America or ask her to come back to Turkey. I was losing my mind from being alone and away from my family all the time. I was not thinking rationally. I called one of my friends to go out to dinner with him. His name was Mehdi too. We sat down at the table to order something to eat. I'd been to this restaurant a couple of times before. I was telling Mehdi that I was tired and could not go any farther. I did not know what I should do.

The café had Wi-Fi connection and while we were talking, I heard a beep from my email. At first, I did not pay any attention to it, but I thought I better check it to see if it was anything important. When I opened the mail, I saw the U.S. Eagle on the top of the page. It was a letter from the American Embassy. I was speechless. I could not believe that it was for real. I was so happy that I jumped up from the table and called Jeyran immediately. She was sleeping, so I called her several times, but she did not answer. I called my mom and told her they asked me to go for an interview at the Embassy the next week and I was going. I hung up and watched my phone to see if Jeyran called me. I was anxious to tell her the great news. I knew she was going to be happy too. After a couple of minutes, she called me. I answered the phone, but before I could say anything, she said, "I know you have good news for me. God told me something big was about to happen." I replied, "Yes. That's right. It happened already. I am going to the Embassy next week. I was so excited that I could not eat my food and just stepped outside to talk with Jeyran. She was crying and I told her, "Yes, Jeyran, it is over. I am coming. I am coming soon."

Two years had passed since I said goodbye to Jeyran at the airport, but this last week before my interview was the worst time I had since that day. Every second seemed like one day and I was counting every minute. The day came and I went to the Embassy. While I was on the bus to Ankara, I was thinking about the time I would have with my family and my kids. I would be seeing my family again after two years. I was wondering how they would react and how I would react when I saw them. I was thinking about my daughter and that I would finally have the chance to touch her and hold her in my arms. I missed Ali and my wife a lot.

The interview was very long, and I was at the Embassy all day. I realized when I was talking with the FBI agent, he was typing every word that was coming out of my mouth. We were going back and forth asking and answering question after question. They asked my entire life history since I was born. I did not know why they wanted so many details, but I was careful to answer all his questions as truthfully as I could remember. They took my photos and my fingerprints. Then they asked me to sit outside in the lobby and wait. Everybody was gone and I was the only person left waiting inside the Embassy when an immigration officer told me to go home and they would call me to let me know what the next step for me would be. I got my bus ticket and started the fourteen hour journey from Ankara back to my city, not knowing how long I would have to wait before I would hear from the Embassy again.

I was still on the bus when I received a call from the Embassy asking me to bring some pictures from our wedding. They wanted those photos by the next morning. I was approaching my city, so, I would immediately have to buy a return ticket to Ankara. I printed some copies of our wedding pictures and waited for the bus leaving for Ankara. I arrived in Ankara late at night and stayed in a hotel. Early the next morning I dropped the pictures at the door of the Embassy. They did not allow me to go inside this time, so I just left the pictures with them and got on a bus to go home. Once again, I was almost home when the Embassy called me again. This time, they wanted my picture for a passport. So, I had to do the same thing and turn right around. As soon as I returned to Ankara, I took my passport pictures, and dropped them at the Embassy. For almost a week I had been going back and forth from my home to the Embassy in Ankara without a rest. I was so exhausted from the travel that I could hardly think. But still I thought it was worth it because I was doing it to be reunited with my family.

This time, I reached all the way home without receiving a call from the Embassy. After resting, I called Jeyran to tell her all that had happened at the Embassy. I was not able to work the entire week of my interviews and visits to the US Embassy in Ankara; I had spent a lot of money on the bus tickets and having to eat outside food. A week later, they sent me a mail with my doctor's appointment. It was in my city, so I did not have to go far. They took my blood to make sure I was healthy and free from drugs. I knew that once they screened my health, the process was almost done. I could sense that my wait was coming to an end and I was starting to get excited. I was getting impatient, counting every minute until I would get my airplane ticket. I was also thinking about my family here – my mom and sisters, and all my friends. I had lived there almost nine years and I had a lot of good memories. I had my ups and downs, my good times and bad; it would be hard to leave all the people and things I loved, but I needed to focus on my future and think of my family waiting for me in America. I remembered from a long time ago that a man had prophesied this moment. He told me, "One day, you will go and live in America." I did not believe it then because there was no sign of help and not even a distant relative that could help me get to America. But now my daughter is an American citizen, and my wife and son live there too. It was amazing how everything came together like pieces of a puzzle. My whole life was about to change.

I passed all my medical tests; they gave me a sealed envelope and instructed me to drop it at the Embassy the next day, which I did. I went back home and waited for the next step. A couple of days later, I received my airplane ticket for America in my email. "Yes," I thought, "it is for real." I looked at that ticket like I had won the lottery. I was so happy that I called Jeyran right away to tell her. After I told her, she asked me hang up and she would call back. I knew what she was doing; she was going to talk with her heavenly Father and give thanks. While she was praying, I was talking to myself, "It is finished. Yes, I am going to America." After two years, I could finally see my family again. I was going to have to say goodbye to my family here, but they understood and were very happy for me.

I wished I had a little money so I could buy some presents for my kids and for Jeyran, but I was broke. The only thing I had of value was my phone but I sold it so I could have some money to travel with. I had no idea what would happen when I got to America, but I knew everything was going to be alright – just as Jeyran told me every day. I did not want my family to come to the airport with me because of the cost and the time. I also knew it would be an emotional scene at the airport like the one I had with Jeyran and Ali when they departed for America. I knew it would be much harder for those left behind than for the one traveling, so I said my goodbyes when I left my city.

The person from the Embassy that I met at the airport brought two other refugee families: one Iranian man and two ladies from Somalia. We were all going to America. The Iranian gentleman was an older man and he was being accompanied by two young men and one girl. I thought they were all going to America, but one of the young men approached me and asked me where I was from. After I told him I was from Afghanistan, he asked me if would please help. The older man was his father and he was traveling alone to New York. He told me his father had a disability and not to let him drink any alcohol on the flight. I was shocked because this was their dad and they wanted me to watch him and keep him from drinking. How was I to order someone old enough to be my own father not to drink? My father never drank alcohol, so I did not know how it was supposed to work for me to tell his dad that. But he was persistent, and I said okay, I would do it for him.

They introduced me to their dad, and we became friends. He was a retired general from the Iranian army. I thought that Iranians were very devout and observed the customs of their religion but this one drank alcohol. As his children requested, I sat down on the seat next to him. And told the waiter, if I fell asleep, please do not serve him any alcohol. They agreed, but in the middle of the night, I woke up and saw a glass of whiskey in his hand and he had been drinking. I asked him what he was doing, and did he not understand that he was sick and should not do that? He gave me his excuse that he had not drank for a long time because his sons would not let him drink while he was staying with them. So, he wanted to enjoy his time now that he was free from his sons' control. I asked him how it was possible for a retired commander in the Iranian Army to be drinking alcohol. I thought all people of his status were religious people. He was telling me stories about his dad and how they lived and what they believed. Finally, I said, "Okay, but only one glass." I did not want to deal with him if he was drunk. But after only one glass he got drunk and was talking very loudly and acting weird. I called the stewardess and asked her who gave him the alcohol to drink. She did not know about my request, but she said this was the last and they would not serve him anymore. I managed to fall back to sleep and when I woke up, we had landed, and it was time to change our airplane. I said goodbye to the old man. He was still drunk and could not walk, but I wished him good luck and departed the plane without him.

Another person assigned to help arriving refugees, came and told me the new place I had to go and the new airplane I need to take. He had my name and all my information. As I was waiting in line for them to check my documents, I looked out the windows of the airport. It was huge; I was sure it was the biggest airport I had ever seen. They told me I had to stay there overnight at a hotel and the next morning I would board an airplane to Georgia. I did not have a phone or any way to communicate with Jeyran. I tried to find a way to call but there was no way. Every time I tried to call it was blocked; there were still strict rules I had to follow.

They moved us to small hotel out of the city, and we spent all night at the hotel. In the morning they came to pick us up and took us back to the airport for one last flight. At last the moment had come and I was on my way for my last trip to be reunited with my family. I was so excited that flight was only 2 or 3 hours long and after that I would see my wife and children. I could not imagine that one day I would be coming to the USA with a Visa – that America would be the first country I could enter without trouble. I remembered the voice that came to my mind when I was in Greece. I went back over in my mind all those bad things that had happened to me on my many journeys, but this final journey was the best of all. Now I knew that somehow all those things that had happened to me along the way had happened for a reason.

CHAPTER NINETEEN

SEEING MY DOUGHTER FIRST TIME

I could hardly contain my excitement as my plane touched down at the airport in Atlanta, Georgia. We transferred from the plane to a bus that took us to the International Terminal. It had been a long flight from Turkey, but my journey was just about at an end. I was impatient to see my family and was counting every second. I looked everywhere, thinking I might be able to see them. It took some time to get through Passport control and baggage claim, but finally, they put me on the train that leads underground from the Terminal to the exit point and the street. Someone from the resettlement agency came and greeted me when I stepped off the train. They knew that someone from

239

my family knew my time of arrival and would pick me up. I went upstairs to the greeting area, but no one was there. I looked all around, but no one was there to greet me. I asked some people if I was at the right place. At last, a young woman approached me and introduced herself. She told me she was my case worker and would help me get my documents and inform me of everything I needed to know. I told her I needed to find my family.

She called Jeyran for me; Jeyran was so excited I was there. She told me they were stuck in a traffic jam but would be there in forty minutes. I was relieved to hear they were on the way and started talking with my case worker to pass the time.

Finally, I heard the voice from behind me calling, "Baba, Baba!" I turned and saw Ali running toward me. He reached out his hands and jumped into my arms. I was overjoyed to see him again. I hugged him and lifted him up. Then I saw Jeyran coming and she was crying and holding Radmila in her arms. I embraced all three of them; I was so happy to see them again. The person who gave them a ride to the airport was recording the moment on video; we all cried for a few minutes and then sat down to talk. We were at a loss for words for a moment or two. I had waited two years to hold Radmila in my arms and just wanted to savor the moment. She was so tiny, and I thought the cutest little girl I had ever seen. She kept pulling herself toward her mom because she did not understand who I was. Even though I kept telling her I was her dad, she was very shy. There are no words I can use to express how happy I was at that moment. Words fail me to describe the pain we went through and the feelings of joy we had the moment we were reunited. I don't think there are any words for it.

We left the airport and Jeyran's friend drove us home – a home I had only seen from a small screen on my phone. I thought I could spend the rest of my time with my family in this home. It was a long drive – about one and a half hours – from the airport to the place where Jeyran and the children had been living. On the way, Jeyran and I exchanged stories of my ride on the airplane and her story of the drive through the traffic to get to the airport. We told each other at the same time, that it was over; we were not going to be apart like this ever again. While we were talking, I was watching the highway; it was the biggest highway I had ever seen in my life. Everywhere I looked there were trees, and everything was green. It looked like Georgia was one, big forest. I told Jeyran that I liked it here already, and she said she liked it too. Jeyran was happy that we were going to live here. She said, "It's a good place to live and the weather is awesome."

When we finally reached home, I discovered it was a dark, basement room. Jeyran pulled up the garage door and invited me inside. I was surprised that there was no other door. Jeyran said the garage door was the door they normally used. I went inside and saw one small bed in the far corner of the room and a small carpet in the middle. It was a cold room with just one TV and a couple of toys for the children. Jeyran had written a lot of prayer notes and stuck them to the walls around the room. I could not sleep that night; we just sat and talked and laughed and cried. We shared the pain we had suffered and the joy we hoped to experience together in the future.

The next night her landlord invited us to their house which was the main part of the house above the garage and basement. They made a big meal for me to welcome me. She was an Iranian woman and lived with her elderly mother. She was a very nice woman and told me how she prayed for Jeyan and for me to come to America. I met a couple other family members and met the family that donated their car to Jeyran. This was a big surprise to me because I had never heard of someone giving their car as a gift to someone else. I felt that my first two nights in America were a good start. The days passed quickly, and we came to the end of the week. Saturday night, Jeyran told me she had arranged some meetings for us in the morning. I asked her what was going on and she said some friends were coming and would take us to church. We did not have driver's licenses, so we could not drive the car.

In the morning a young man came to the door and introduced himself. His name was Amir and he was from Iran. He was a handsome young man with black eyes, black hair, and a well-trimmed beard. He looked like a typical Iranian gentleman. He was a driver and helped us with the car seat and all things we needed in the car for the ride to the church. It took almost an hour to reach the church. When we arrived in the church parking lot I was in for another surprise. It was a huge parking lot and a lot of people were walking toward the entrance of the church. In the crowd were all kinds of people: black, white, and Hispanic. I could hear them speaking in English, Spanish, and other languages I did not know. When we walked up to the front doors, a couple of men and an old lady were standing there. They greeted us and held the door open for us as we stepped inside the church. I felt welcomed and walked right into the church.

Inside, I could hear the voices of women singing and followed Jeyran into a large hall where a lot of people were sitting. Jeyran told me the worship had just started. When we sat down, I saw several people coming and saying something to Jeyran. I could tell that they were asking if I was her husband and they all said they were happy to see me. One woman approached me and told me I was an answer to their prayers. I asked her what she meant, but she did not say anything and went away. The doors closed and the lights went off. Then a woman started singing. As soon as I heard the first part of that song, I fell in love with that worship music. The woman was singing "You are a good, good Father." She had a beautiful voice and I loved what she was singing. When we sat down, the Pastor came to the stage and the first thing he did was announced my name and asked me to stand. I stood up and everybody clapped their hands for me. I was shy and did not know what I should say.

Jeyran had told me that the Pastor would preach for about thirty five minutes and then the service would end. After his sermon, the Pastor came up to me and gave me a hug. His wife, children, and other members of the church came to meet me and welcomed me to the church and to America. After everyone was gone, the Pastor and his family took us out to lunch. My first visit to the church went great. I liked the church and appreciated the friends and family we had there. I was wondering how I could possibly thank all of them for protecting and loving my family all the time I was not able to be here for them.

I had to immediately start looking for a job and learn how to make money in America. We would have to move closer to the city. The guy who was giving us rides to church every Sunday found an apartment in the same complex where he was living. After we moved there, I found a job at a car dealership with the help of another friend of Jeyran's. Someone would come and pick me up every morning and drop me off every night. It was a hard job, cleaning trash from the yard and trees. I had to trash everything I could see that did not belong on the ground. But I had no complaints. I had done harder work than that.

I showed everyone that I was ready to work and to prove to everyone that I would do a good job.

As the days passed, I was interacting with more and more of Jeyran's friends. All were friendly to me, but I knew that all of them were hoping that one day I would start following Jesus. That may have been their dream for me, but it was not mine. I never thought that one day I would turn away from my dad and our ancestors. I had a lot of questions in my mind about their beliefs, but I was scared to share them with others. I even kept my questions from Jeyran because I knew she was thinking the same way as her friends, but before we got married, we had an agreement not to talk about our beliefs. Each of us would be free to follow our own beliefs. But serious questions started coming into my mind after I saw how strongly they reacted when I made a joke about their beliefs and started asking some odd questions about how Jesus could possibly be the Son of God. In my faith, the idea that Jesus is

God's Son is not something we can accept. Muslims did not believe that God had a partner. You cannot see God or touch Him, so how can He have a Son? I was getting different answers, but none of them were convincing enough for me to understand that concept.

I was close to two guys, Amir and Bahar. They lived in the apartment upstairs and we saw them almost every day. One day I had to go somewhere with Jeyran to do some paperwork, but I could not find them to help us with a ride. While we were waiting for them to show up, I was talking with Jeyran and sharing my experience with her. I told her that I liked how her friends were acting towards me. I was very grateful to meet them, and I liked that they did not talk about their religion; they did not try to force me to believe the same way they did. But unconsciously, I had been comparing their behavior with other people I had known in my life-time. I saw how easy it was for people in my past to carry a grudge against me, and how often I would carry a grudge against anyone who crossed me or did me wrong. But I had to admit to myself that it was less an issue about them than it was about my-self and how I treated others. I saw how I often treated others with suspicion, questioned their motives, and quickly assumed the worst in them.

I wondered if something was not right in me and I needed to find out what it was. Did people like Amir and Bahar change because they lived in America; or because they believed something different? Muslims believe that Mohammad is the only true prophet and that Islam is the best religion in the world. Why, then is my country and so many other Muslim countries in the world in trouble all the time? They always blame it on others and think all their problems are someone else's fault – especially America and Israel. Now that I was in America, I could see how they helped us improve our lives. They find us jobs and give us encouragement. I had never in my life before had people help me the way these people had done.

I was afraid to ask these questions out loud because in my heart I felt that maybe if I asked them, they would think I wanted to change my beliefs. I did not want to get in conversations with anybody about what I was thinking or feeling, but my mind was full of questions and I was trying to be honest with myself about what the answers meant. I started to doubt my past; question after question was coming to my mind and I could not stop them. Finally, I opened my mind enough to have some short conversations with my friends about the Bible. They told me most people have questions about Bible and they try to find problems with the Bible, but you are different, you honestly look at your problems and try to find the Bible's answers to them.

Every Sunday and a couple of days every week we were going to Bible study or church. We had fun and good times of fellowship with people from our church. I was slowly moving closer to the point of following Jesus, but whenever one of my friends opened a conversation with me about my beliefs and faith, I told them, "I don't have any problems with Christianity or Jesus. I am attending church and Bible study, but if Jesus wants me to follow Him, He needs to come and talk to me. I need to see something that tells me Jesus is real, otherwise, I cannot believe."

I had heard people talking about having visions and dreams, but I wondered how it could be possible. I did not believe that God spoke to people that way. They quoted this verse from Jeremiah 1:5, "Before I formed you in the womb, I knew you; before you were born, I set you apart..." and I could not believe that either. Then one night I had a dream that was different. I saw my cousin (his name is Mehdi too) in my dream. I was sitting in a dark room and Mehdi opened the door and a man came inside. I looked at his face; I recognized him, and he greeted me. Then he gave me a box. I asked him what it was, and he told me it was a gift for me from him. I was surprised and opened it. I saw a piece of wood in the box, took it out, and turned it around.

I could see it was a cross and my eyes opened wider. I was surprised because I got this gift from a person who is a strict Muslim. I did not know what it meant.

I remembered very well that Mehdi is a strict Muslim because in 2002, I went to visit their house in Afghanistan. It was the first time in my life I had been to Afghanistan and I had gone there to see all my cousins and my father's sister and her husband. My first day there, they were happy to see me. But after the second day, their behavior changed. They started bringing food to my door and would not allow me to eat food with them. They would not call me to get together and sit and talk with them. I was hurt and angry by the way they were treating me. I called my cousin Mehdi and asked him what was going on. He told me his father called me an infidel because I did not wake up early in the morning and pray like a Muslim. His father said I was dirty and so they would not allow them to eat food with me and wanted me to stay in my room.

I said okay, I understood, but that is normal in my family and nobody said anything to me about it. But if it made everyone happy, I would start praying like a good Muslim starting the next morning. But my cousin said, "Not from tomorrow, start praying today. Right now." I said, "Okay" and started praying. But I was not praying all those prayers for God; I was doing them because I wanted them to accept me in their house. All our prayers are in Arabic and I don't understand what I am praying anyway. After a couple of days of praying regularly, it became too much. I searched and found one of my uncles and moved into his house.

After that I did not see Mehdi anymore. I knew he was living in New York now and was getting his PhD. I did not know but after that dream, I thought maybe he was in touch with some Christians too.

I did not understand the meaning of my dream, but I told it to my neighbor, to my pastor's wife Carrie, and to Jeyran. All of them told me something was about to happen in my life. I was wondering what that was and was impatient to find out. We went to church the next Sunday and everything was the same. Pastor Carrie led the worship with her amazing voice. I don't remember what her husband preached, but I remember feeling like my whole body was under the conviction of the Holy Spirit. I was thinking all Sunday and the next day about the dream and something the pastor said in his sermon. When I got back to work, I was alone in the shop and working on an old car. It was normal for me to come in early in the morning and start working to learn something new. But that day was not going to be a typical day. I vividly remember that moment – even the car's year, make, and model – two of its lug nuts were broken and there was no way to take them off.

I was feeling different and was still waiting to see if anything big was going to happen. Suddenly, I felt something turning me around; I heard nothing, but it felt like a tornado lifted me up and turned me around like a leaf in the wind. I was so scared that I did not know what to do. I heard a voice from within telling me that I was not here for this job. (Even now, as I am typing this on my keyboard, describing that moment, my body is shivering.) A few seconds after I heard that voice, everything was back to normal. But I was so frightened by what had happened that I did not return to that place for two days. That night, on the day it happened I shared with Jeyran what I had experienced. She told me again that something was about to happen, and to just watch and see. I asked her what she meant by that and I told her she was scaring me. She reminded me that I had said that I would not believe in the God of the Bible unless He came and spoke to me. "There He is!" she said. Still I could not believe that it was God talking to me. Jeyran said, "Yes, listen to all the people around you. You think all of them are suffering from delusions, or that they are lying. No, this is real, and He wants to talk to you. Listen to His voice and hear what He is saying."

The next day at work, my boss told me there was an old car in the yard that needed to go to the body shop to be repaired. He wanted me to drive it there. It was part of my job to drive cars to the body shop. So, it was nothing unusual and I did it almost every workday. It was an old Honda Civic that made a lot of noise when I started driving it. When I got it on the highway and started going faster, noise was coming from everywhere under the hood of the car. I was thinking that the car engine was overheating and I needed to go faster to allow the air to cool it. So, I pressed the gas pedal and accelerated to 70 miles per hour. It was scary to drive that old car so fast, but I felt something was breaking with the car and I needed to get it to the repair shop as fast as I could.

Speeding down the highway, I started feeling the way I did the other morning in the shop and the same voice came to my mind telling me to turn off the radio and listen to Him. I turned off the radio and was ready to listen. But I felt a second voice coming into my mind, confusing me. One voice was saying "Listen to Me." And the other was saying, "faster, faster" and I did not know which one I needed to listen to. Suddenly, there was a big noise right in front of the car. I felt something hit me in the face; there was smoke everywhere and I could not see a thing in front of me. I could hear people blowing their horns, but at first, I could not see what had happened. Then I realized that the front hood of the car had come loose, hit the windshield, and smashed it. I was able to maintain control of the car and pulled over to the side of the road. My face was bloody and there was glass everywhere in my hair and clothes. I was stunned and confused. I called someone to pick me up and they towed the car away. When I got back home, I shared with Jeyran what had happened. I did not understand what was going on. I was thinking that I did not have this much drama in my life when I was smuggling people, but today I heard two different voices telling me different things. All Jeyran could tell me was that something was about to happen, but I still did not know what it was.

I was so shaken up by the accident that I took a couple of days off from work to recover. All these things had happened to me in a two-week period and I was worried about what could happen to me next. I felt that something was pushing me, and my heart did not feel the same as before. I really felt I needed to change something instead of waiting for something to change. I was thinking all day and all night about my past and my future. I reflected upon everything I had done and acknowledged that I was a sinner and there was no chance to be saved in my religion. One night Jeyran was over in our neighbor's house and I was alone. The kids were sleeping and was laying on the bed and thinking about everything when I heard the door open and Jeyran came inside. I wanted to talk with Jeyran about what I was feeling and asked her to close the door. I told her I wanted to talk to her about something.

I told her, "You see everything that is happening in my life and it affects you too. I could not sleep all night and all day. I cannot concentrate on my job either. I have a question. If I believe Jesus tonight, what do I have to do?" She held my hands and started crying. She said she did not want anything else in her life, just that I would be saved. "This is all my prayers since we were married, and I really don't want you to stay like you were. I want you to change and I am sure God's message is He has something for you. That's why He brought you here. Not for your daughter. God called you and you are here. You are not here to become a mechanic or something else. You are here for a purpose and he did not bring you all the way here and saved you from all those dangerous situations to leave you alone." We looked into each other's eyes and held each other's hands, and I said, "Okay."

Jeyran started crying and said she was so happy. She ran out to find some of our neighbors so they could read a specific prayer for me, but all of them were sleeping. Finally, we found one of our friends and he agreed to come and read the prayer for me. He opened the Bible and asked me to repeat after him. I opened my heart and asked Jesus to come into my heart and my life – to save me and direct my life from that moment on. And finished the prayer with "Amen."

When I woke up the next day, I started seeing the world differently. I saw my wife and kids differently. I felt like some heavy weight was removed from my shoulders. My heart felt so fresh and clean and every breath I took was refreshing and made me feel good inside.

CHAPTER TWENTY

BECOME CITIZENS OF HEAVEN

It has been five years since I asked Jesus into my life. A short time after I became a believer, I was invited by my church to share my testimony. I have been happy to share my story many times. But one day some questions were asked by one of my church members that changed my mindset and perspective completely. She asked me, "Since you first believed in Jesus and gave your heart to Him, what has happened in your life and how has Jesus impacted your life? Is anything changed?" It started me thinking that I had a lot to say about how I became a Christian, but I did not think about how to talk about sharing how my life had changed since that day.

My life has changed since I became a follower of Jesus. The greatest change I can share is how different my behavior has become. Looking back on my testimony, explains a lot about my personality. I was full of anger, revenge, and hate. I don't blame anyone for that; I was raised in an environment of hate. Living as refugees from Afghanistan in Iran caused a lot of people to hate my father and his family. Ethnic and religious hatred were everywhere and often determined how I was treated. Most important of all, my previous relationship with God caused me to only know Him as one who punished those who did not obey. I only knew a hard-hearted God who would never forgive my mistakes or trespasses. My faith was measured by my deeds; in Islam, God only wants you to make sacrifices for him and do good works to turn away his wrath. Early in my life, I realized I could not do enough to please God and fell away from God because I felt I was not a good Muslim and was not perfect. So, I gave up all together.

I started loving money because it was giving me power. Even my family respected me more because I was able to help them and bring some happiness – at least temporarily. After I got married to Jeyran, I brought my way of life with me. I was very strict with Ali for even the small mistakes that all three year old children make. I was raising him the way I had been raised and showed him the same unforgiveness that life had taught me. None of that bothered me because I was just being who I thought I should be. I was happy to intimidate my family and make them afraid of me because that was I how I could get them to obey me and do whatever I told them to do.

Even after I accepted Jesus in my life, my behavior toward my family did not change. I was going to church and sharing my testimony and saying, "Hallelujah", "God bless you", and "praise the Lord" – all those words I had learned from going to church. I was thinking that was all I needed to do. I professed, "I am a Christian," and was doing great. But believing in Jesus only made me have two faces. Something was wrong with my perspective and understanding of the Bible. I took the concept of "grace" out of context. I held the idea that now I was saved, and God forgave my sins, whatever I did, God would forgive. I was free because Jesus died for me and I am forgiven. So, I could wear my real face at home and my fake face at church; I could act like I was a good person and all spiritual, while nothing had changed in my heart. But all that was about to change.

One day, while I was at work, I received a call from Ali's school. They told me it was reported to them that when my son was in the school bus on the way home, he told a bad word to the girls inside the bus. I was so angry, I wanted to leave work right away, find Ali and punish him severely – the best way I knew how. But my boss told me I had to stay and work until the end of my shift at 5 o'clock. I had been invited to church that night by a friend who knew I was an ex-Muslim. He found my testimony interesting enough to share in their church, but I was telling myself I had to leave and go home to give my son the "blessing" he deserved. Then I would go to church and say all the things I had to say about how I got saved.

I still thought I was a spiritual person and that I was no different from most people who must be acting like they were spiritual in public, but in real life they were not that kind of person. (If you are that kind of person, then please read to the end because the thing I am going to share with you is the way God can change your life. God changes us not by force or pushing us, but by His love.) After work, I went to the church and met my friend brock. We were talking together about things in general until the service was ready to start. I was sitting all the way in the corner when they turned the lights off and the pastor came out to preach. He started preaching about Jesus' crucifixion. He had done some research about his struggle and suffering on the cross. He was describing Jesus' crucifixion in a clear and powerful way. He demonstrated the pain Jesus must have felt from the nails in His hands and feet and how His body was broken from being beaten and nailed on the cross. After about ten minutes, he paused and asked, "Do you know why I told you all this? It is because this man, this great man, He is God and is the only Son of God." Then he read John 3:16, "For God so loved the world that he gave his one and only Son, that whoever believes in him shall not perish but have eternal life."

He went on to say that the only thing He asked you to do... then he paused and came toward the place where I was sitting and pointed his finger toward me and said, "Go home. Jesus is telling you to go home and hug your son and tell him you love him, the way Jesus loved you." (Even now, as I am typing this, I cannot stop crying.) I was full of anger and suddenly, the moment he pointed his finger at me and continued preaching, I felt something change in my heart.

I thought about all that had happened that day. I started crying and they suddenly turned the lights back on. My friend sitting next to me, saw my face and he asked me what happened to me. I told him I should leave. I could not sit there any longer. He followed me out of the church and I told him what had happened that day and after I left the church I was going to go home and punish my son, but this preacher pointed his finger at me, and even though he did not know who I was – he told me to go home and love my son. I saw him starting to cry and he told me, "Let me share my small story that changed my life." He was stealing things when he was a child. One day he was caught, and the police came to his house. His dad had been severely punishing him the same way I was doing to my son. And when the police left, he went to his dad's bedroom and pulled the leather belt from his pants and brought it to his dad. He told him, "Dad, this is your belt; punish me as you wish." But his father

put down the belt and hugged him and told him he
forgave him. He said, "Son, don't do it anymore."
My friend looked me in the eyes and said, "Mehdi,
that day was the last time in my life that I stole anything. I did not stop because the police came or because I was ashamed. I did it because I did not want
to embarrass my dad again." Then my friend told
me the same thing, "Go home and forgive your
son."

I was thinking all the way home. When I arrived, I saw Ali was shaking and Jeyran was afraid
of what I was about to do. I told Ali to go to his
room. Jeyran looked at me asked me not to beat
him. I told Jeyran I wanted to tell them something.
We went into Ali's room together and he was sitting. As soon as he saw me, he put his hands on his
face and started shaking and going away from me. I
told him, "Come here son. I don't want to do it.
Come I want to hug you. I love you." He could not
believe it. He thought I was trying to trick him, but I
reached out to him and hugged him. Then we all
started crying. I asked him to forgive me for all the
things I had done to him. I promised him I would
not do it anymore. Then Ali told me that he loved
me.

After that day our relationship has gotten stronger and his behavior in school changed drastically. Now I understand the power of forgiveness. And the most important thing is how God loves me and how powerful is the love of God. As Paul said in 1 Corinthians 13, love never fails and the greatest gift from God is love. As you have learned from my story, I am not scared of a lot of things. Today, I am stronger and wiser, but I am afraid of embarrassing my heavenly Father because of my actions. I am not afraid He will reject me or severely punish me because He forgave me on the cross already. I am afraid of embarrassing Him because He loves me so much and I love Him so much that I do not want to hurt him. Discovering and walking in God's love is the best journey I have ever been on. If you have read this book, my hope and prayer for you is that you will discover as I did that God is real and He cares about you as a person. God can change your life from the inside. He wants to change your heart and so change you into a new creation. "Therefore, if anyone is in Christ, he is a new creation; old things have passed away; behold, all things have become new." 2 Corinthians 5:17

THE END

EDITOR'S NOTE

FRED & DEENA OSBORN

When my wife first handed the file containing Mehdi's story to me, I must confess that I was not looking forward to opening it and editing it. I was in the process of putting the finishing touches on my latest book, a commentary on the book of Revelation, and looking at Mehdi's story was not something that I thought would interest me very much. But once I was able to give his story my full attention, I became completely captivated by the account of his life on the refugee trail that led him from Iran to the West and freedom. As I read his tale, I became fascinated with every detail. I hung on every cliff with him as he trekked through the snowy mountain trails of Iran. I felt his pain and loneliness in Turkey and wanted to be there with him to encourage him in those times when all seemed lost and he wanted to give up. I could almost feel the fears he had to overcome as he faced wild animals, crossed the sea in a small boat, and dodged the police that were always on the lookout for illegal refugees that dared to step from the shadows or seek justice. I was impressed by the courage of this young refugee and found myself wanting to push ahead of my edited pages to see what would happen to him next and find out how he made it to America.

His story is not a pretty one. For a while, he became a human smuggler, taking advantage of those who were once in his same predicament. For a long time, he lived outside of the law. He lied, cheated, stole, and bribed his way through many situations while thousands of illegal dollars flowed through his hands.

At one point his body was shattered and he was near death. But through it all, I could sense the unseen hand of God protecting him and leading him through. It would not be until near the end of the part of his life's story told here that Mehdi was able to see for himself who it was that had been directing his path all along. But in the end, the physical and spiritual journeys he traveled merged into one. Today, Mehdi and his family have come out of the shadows and live in the light of freedom. It has been my honor and a great blessing to help him tell his story.